SCENES FROM

SCENES FROM A DISTURBED CHILDHOOD

Adam Czerniawski

SERPENT'S
TAIL

Library of Congress Catalog Card Number: 91-61199

British Library Cataloguing in Publication Data
Czerniawski, Adam
  Scenes from a disturbed childhood
  I. Title
  920
  ISBN 1-85242-241-6

First published 1991 by
Serpent's Tail, 4 Blackstock Mews, London N4 and
401 West Broadway # 2, New York, NY 10012

Typeset in Aster 10/13pt by AKM Associates UK Ltd, Southall,
London

Printed by Cox & Wyman Limited of Reading, Berkshire

CONTENTS

ACKNOWLEDGEMENTS

The quotations in chapter 1 are taken from: *Wrzesień 1939 w relacjach dyplomatów*[September 1939 Through the Eyes of Diplomats] ed. Andrzej Skrzypek, Warsaw 1989; *Poland and the Coming of the Second World War. The diplomatic papers of A.J. Drexel Biddle Jr.*, ed. Philip V. Cannistraro et al., Columbus 1976; and *Dziennik* [Diary] by Wacław Lipiński, Warsaw 1989.

I am indebted to Kazimierz Bosek for his research into my mother's family history.

The cover illustration prepared from a photograph by Michał Sielewicz is *Promień Słońca* [Sunbeam] by Tadeusz Makowski, reproduced by kind permission of the National Museum of Warsaw and with the co-operation of Andrzej Januszewicz, Director of the Authors' Agency.

My incidental comments, explanations and translations inserted into quoted material are enclosed in square brackets.

'Pan', 'Pani' and 'Panna' are Polish for Mr, Mrs and Miss respectively. 'Adaś', 'Kazio', 'Kacio' and 'Rozunia' are the diminutives of Adam, Kazimierz, Konstanty and

Rozetka. Polish surnames ending in 'ki' are masculine gender – the feminine ending is 'ka'.

The route taken by the diplomats during their retreat from Warsaw and our own escape routes are indicated on the map on p.ix.

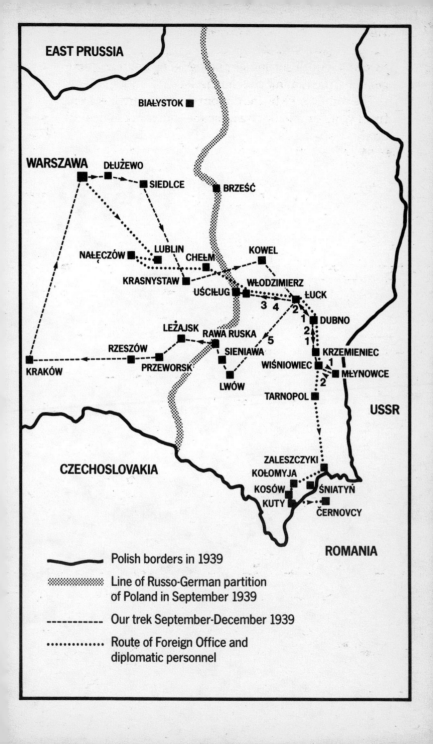

EAST PRUSSIA

BIAŁYSTOK ■

WARSZAWA
DŁUŻEWO ■
■ SIEDLCE
BRZEŚĆ ■

KOWEL ■

NAŁĘCZÓW ■ LUBLIN ■
CHEŁM ■
WŁODZIMIERZ
KRASNYSTAW ■ UŚCIŁUG ■ ■ ■ ŁUCK
3 4 2
1 ■ DUBNO
LEŻAJSK ■ 2
RAWA RUSKA ■ 1
RZESZÓW ■ ■ SIENIAWA 5 ■ KRZEMIENIEC
KRAKÓW ■ ■ PRZEWORSK WIŚNIOWIEC ■ 1 ■ MŁYNOWCE
LWÓW ■ 2
TARNOPOL ■

USSR

CZECHOSLOVAKIA

ZALESZCZYKI ■
KOŁOMYJA ■
KOSÓW ■ ■ ŚNIATYŃ
KUTY ■ ČERNOVCY ■

ROMANIA

━━━ Polish borders in 1939

▒▒▒▒ Line of Russo-German partition
of Poland in September 1939

------ Our trek September–December 1939

.... Route of Foreign Office and
diplomatic personnel

Is it more painful to recall a childhood that has vanished cataclysmically or a childhood that fades away gradually within an orderly progress of time?

Józef Zenon Tynicki

Human nature being what it is, every autobiography is inescapably mendacious.

Ernesto Sábato

INTRODUCTION

I

I was nearly five years old when the Second World War started. I was old enough to realise what was happening, yet young enough to experience 1939 and the succeeding years of my war-time and post-war childhood in a totally different way from that of the adults: soldiers, politicians, writers, victims of atrocities and concentration camps, who are the authors of most of the autobiographical material of those years.

I had an early awareness that my experiences were very special also because they seemed different from the standard Polish experiences which divided fairly neatly into: (1) escape to the West and army service with the allies, (2) deportation to Soviet labour camps, and (3) survival under German occupation.

My desire to chronicle the family adventures crystallised relatively recently and grew very gradually. For years I urged my mother to record the events on paper. She jotted down a few recollections which I have reproduced here; she would have been much better with a microphone, but that didn't occur to me early enough. There were additionally, and much more importantly, bundles of mother's letters and postcards, a few of my sister's (some crucial ones lost, seemingly in the post between Warsaw and Bucharest) and mother's random diary notes for 1942–52. For years I took no interest in the postcards, except as a stamp collector, which prompted me to vandalise some of the cards for stamps that the Germans had introduced and which were, one has to admit, remarkably beautiful. Clearing out my parents' flat after father's death in 1971, I was close – I recall with horror – to throwing these bundles away.

I have woven extracts from these documents into my narrative for two main reasons: (1) they are remarkable on their own account and (2) they offer a different perspective to mine. In an important sense it was fortunate that I remained ignorant of the content of these records until I had produced the first outline of the story entirely from my own memory.

Moreover, recording my own version of events I was uneasily conscious that I might, in large part, be reproducing my mother's vivid and graphic verbal accounts. But subsequent examination of her and my sister's correspondence convinced me that this was not the case. There was nothing in my direct experience to match mother's sense of terror, despair and desolation; and if my sister was a sharp observer of the comic trivia which seem an inevitable part of tragedy, her perspective was different from mine.

Inevitably, the adults saw the situation in wider, political terms. However, the correspondence reaching father from Warsaw was subject to strict censorship (even the stamp had to be licked in the presence of an official in case one was tempted to insert a micro-message beneath it), hence its totally apolitical nature. Only mother's reference to documentation proving our non-Jewish origins chillingly hints at the horrors to come. This was the reason for my bringing in voices of people who had a broader appreciation of the September events and were able to comment on them as they evolved. The fact that some of these witnesses were closely associated with my family and that they followed much the same route in their flight east, made the inclusion of their testimonies especially relevant.

I am not claiming that what I present as my own narrative is an exact portrayal of my experiences and thoughts over half a century ago. Apart from the inaccuracies and failures of my own memory – admittedly always good but fraying somewhat at the edges in recent years – there is the question of how much of mother's subsequent reminiscing was absorbed into and altered my memories – I now refer to the facts, rather than the mood, on which I comment above. Clearly, such a process must have taken place. But again, on the written evidence, I am struck by how much of the narrative which I claim as genuinely my own is so. Many of these memories simply find no counterpart in the two women's accounts and where there is convergence or overlap, the nuances and slight differences are striking. Striking, because they reassure me that my memory (being that of a very young child) is not necessarily less reliable than theirs, and that at times it proves superior. Three examples: (1) my mother recalls (years later) that the man in the forest who gave us all such a fright, was carrying a scythe. I never doubted that he was carrying a saw and this fact I regard as conclusively confirmed by my sister recording the event only three months after it happened; (2) similarly, I had no doubt that some of our night trekking in December 1939 took place in moonlight, and that (3) earlier on, during our flight from Warsaw, we had stopped in Lublin. Reading a draft of my memoir in 1989, my sister insisted that we did not travel through Lublin and that the nights in the forest were pitch-dark. However, mother's recollections quite emphatically confirm the Lublin route, while my sister's own letters, written at the time, are equally insistent on moonlit nights. Because our trek lasted about a week, and we three all agree that some nights were pitch-

black, it is reasonable to suppose that fifty years later
my sister remembers only the incidents that took place
on moonless nights.

The only significant way in which the family documents have caused me to revise my original outline
concerns dates and sequences of events. Overall, my
memory tended to telescope events. I had no awareness
of spending several weeks (rather than a few days) in
Dubno; I had forgotten that father had re-established
contact with us much earlier than I got accustomed to
believing. The dates made available by the correspondence also enabled me to give the narrative a more
cohesive, orderly structure. As to the precise date of
our flight from Warsaw – that remains uncertain.

In weaving others' narratives into mine I was not
aiming at total smoothness, which in any event would
have been impossible to achieve unless I were willing to
embroider the account here and there. While this
method leads to occasional repetitions, gaps and
obscurities, it will, I hope, reassure the reader that I
have attempted to get as close to the truth as possible.

II

My desire to write a memoir was growing in intensity
during the 1980s but I was impeded by uncertainties:
should I write it in Polish or in English? For a bilingual
writer, who however reserves his most intimate writing
(poetry) for the Polish language, Polish seemed the
obvious choice. On the other hand, English had its
attraction in providing a welcome translucent veil
between my personal story and the readers I was about
to take into my confidence. It was also clear to me that,
whichever language I chose, I would follow this up with

a similar exercise in the other language, and that this would not be a straightforward translation: in addressing myself to these two readerships I would have to put on slightly different voices, contract some accounts and expand others, place the emphasis differently here and there, explain to one group what would be all too obvious to the other.

It was Maria Balińska who stirred me from these dogmatic slumbers and to her I owe a special debt of gratitude. When working as a BBC Radio 3 producer, and having already commissioned some literary work from me, she fastened on a chance remark of mine about my childhood years. I was asked to complete three 20-minute scripts within a month. That concentrated my mind wonderfully: the language and the format were chosen for me with no time for doubts and prevarications. I had no idea whether I could squeeze thirteen years of my very eventful childhood into three short talks, but it worked and the broad outline, the synopsis, so to speak, of a larger work was put together. But I still wasn't sure whether there was going to be a larger work. Family and friends were urging me on, and again I was fortunate. Marsha Rowe and Pete Ayrton of Serpent's Tail heard my broadcasts and, with the help of Michael March, got in touch with me to offer publication of my story in book-length form. Once more, a definite structure and timetable were imposed upon a project which otherwise might have lingered at the back of my mind for years.

And had it lingered much longer, it might have proved beyond retrieval. Have I then chosen the optimal moment? Possibly. Earlier, I was too close to the events, too self-conscious to handle them without embarrassment. Later, if not exactly forgotten, they would have acquired the status of myth or legend – so distant and so strange as to require a very formal presentation in a language more suited to ritual than to family history. Of course, earlier on I would have been able to consult my mother (her memory is now no longer serviceable) and earlier still, my father. This is an irretrievable loss; on the other hand, their brooding presence over my narrative would have intimidated me, drained my confidence and eventually even perhaps paralysed my will to proceed. Father felt very confident he could, and should, rewrite my poems to their immense advantage, so he would have been more than ready to rewrite my story, which was, after all, in large part, his story as well. And it is quite possible I would not have had access to the family documents I have used here. My parents were always reticent about discussing family matters in my presence.

There is another discovery I made about writing an autobiography. This concerns its tone and mood. When I finally sat down to composing it, I found myself committed to realism with a dash of epic heroism, piety and humour. I realised, however, that, especially if written at an earlier time, the story would have been shot through with anger, bitterness and resentment. When I was once asked whether this was my first attempt at autobiography, I found the question absurd – surely, there is only one life to describe. But yet it could be described at different levels of awareness. Perhaps this is what my questioner had in mind. But I don't suppose I shall be inclined to go over the same ground in a different mood. Many of the memories recorded here are painful enough not to be dwelt on excessively. Moreover, now that the tale is told, I no longer remember it that clearly – I have to rely on what I have written!

III

Throughout my life I had to fit my writing into the available free moments. While these conditions were frustrating, they were bearable: it was possible to fit the writing of small-scale pieces like poems, essays and short stories into these routines. The prospect of completing under similar conditions a full-length book, which additionally required painstaking examination and transcription of the family archive, was very daunting. And again I was lucky. In 1989 and 1990 I was able to spend a total of six months at the Writers' Retreat at Hawthornden Castle, first as Acting Administrator, then as Fellow.

So I am particularly pleased to record my great gratitude to Mrs Drue Heinz, the creator and Director of the Retreat, and Lord Quinton, the Chairman of its Selection Committee, for making the Retreat available to me at a time when I had most need of it. During my spell as Administrator, Judy Mooney in London and the staff at the castle, led by Effie Thomson and Margaret Allan, made sure that I had time left to work on this book; and on my return as Fellow I was under the care of Dr Joseph McAleer, who spared no effort to uphold the tradition of the Retreat as an ideal working place for those seriously engaged on writing projects.

IV

The admirable Aristotle wisely observes that a story should have a beginning, a middle and an end. Admittedly, that sounds like a banal truth, and applied to an autobiography, suggests a narration covering the period from birth to death. But no one can observe his

Adam Czerniawski

birth or watch his funeral. Where to start, where to end the autobiographical tale? Aristotle of course was attending to the shapeliness of literary works, specifically drama, and there can be a temptation to turn one's life story into a literary artefact, to pretend that one is perpetually burning with a gem-like flame. However, a life is a life and not a work of art. (Quite early on mother began calling me 'the aesthete', so the temptation to play the part was strong.) Artistically, one has little control over it, particularly over one's childhood years. From this point of view, it is fortunate that the most interesting part of my life is its early years: these are the years best suited to objective chronicling before the author has become self-conscious, vain and self-regarding. So two important reasons conspired to make me conclude the story on the brink of maturity.

V

I dedicate this chronicle to Ann, Irena, Fiona, Richard, Stefan and Edward Jacek, who entered my family life after the sequence of events here described. Maybe in another fifty years' time I shall feel able to record this successive period of my life. When I was forty and living with my wife and two growing children in a comfortable Victorian house in an old British provincial city, I became intensely aware of the fact that in 1939 my parents were in their forties with two young children, and I tried to imagine how we would have coped if a war like that had started again in 1974.

Hawthornden Castle, October–November, 1990

PART ONE

Poland

(September 1939 – July 1941)

CHAPTER 1

Pre-existence

Our spacious flat is in the very centre of Warsaw, but feels cosy and secluded. It forms half of an upper storey of an elegant honey-coloured building set at right angles to Nowogrodzka Street, with a long tree-lined vista towards St Barbara's church where I had been christened Adam Józef Zenon. The clinic where I was born in December 1934 is round the corner in Aleje Jerozolimskie, overlooking Warsaw's main railway station with the tracks excitingly hidden underground whence billows of smoke escape at intervals. The house overlooks warehouses that belong to the Polish Tobacco Monopoly of which my father is a director in charge of tobacco purchases abroad. Beyond the warehouses, along Nowogrodzka Street, is the distinctive tall modern building housing the post office; in the opposite direction, backing onto our house, is the Roma cinema, and beyond it, the terminus of the blue-coloured suburban railway which runs in the middle of the street like a tram. At bedtime the hypnotic refrain 'niebieska kolejka, niebieska kolejka' [blue railway, blue railway] gets mixed up with my evening prayers.

The focus of the flat is an opulent drawing room with deep-blue armchairs and sofas, a black upright piano and two oil paintings of my mother: one depicts her in a shiny white gown with a fan; in the other, by Jan Rudnicki, she is sombre in black. There is also a large watercolour portrait of my sister Zosia, seven years my senior, and a series of small reproductions of Michałowski's depictions of Napoleon's campaigns. There are dramatic portrayals of battles and marches through forbidding mountain passes, and of course of the legendary Polish cavalry regiment's suicidal charge at Samosierra in the Peninsular campaign against Wellington.

The flat easily accommodates my parents, my sister, my bachelor uncle Konstanty, my sister's German governess Emma (to whom my father has recently given a copy of *Mein Kampf* to read), my nanny Panna Władysława, whom I call 'Myszka' ['Mousie'], the kitchen staff and a sleek little black dachshund-type mongrel Rozetka (Rozunia) which my sister wheedled out of a farm-labourer during a holiday in the country.

My parents had met at the end of the First World War in Żytomierz when Marshal Piłsudski's newly constituted Polish Army pursued the Red Army deep into the Ukraine and mother greeted the victorious Polish Legions at the head of the local girl guide companies. Father had joined the Legions as a youth in Kraków at their inception. During the closing stages of the First World War this army succeeded in winning Poland's independence from Russia, Prussia and Austria who had occupied the country for over a hundred years.

Mother was born in the Ukraine in Mała Szkarafka [The Little Decanter]. At school the official language was Russian and it left her able to recite Pushkin and Lermontov from memory and (in theory) to pray for the Czar's wellbeing from the tiny Polish-Russian prayer book she always had by her. Polish poetry smuggled into the classroom had the taste of forbidden fruit. Her father was a landowner in a region which included Polish gentry, Ukrainian peasants, Armenian merchants and Jewish shopkeepers. The Russian Revolution had set these groups against each other and grandfather had to flee, saved from a lynch mob by the local Jewish pharmacist and mother's quick-witted deceptions. He had buried the family treasure on the Beżów estate in Szepetówka (maybe it's still there) and took with him bundles of Czarist banknotes which became worthless overnight.

Mother's family, the Tynicki clan, had its roots in central Poland, and is related to the family of Jan Kochanowski, the Renaissance poet. In 1656 'The noble Piotr of Tynica, Janików, Glinica, Wistka and Żapiowo, and lord of the Great Skrzyn, son of Grzegorz and Anna born Tynicka ... raised this monument [in the Skrzyńsko parish church] to remind his descendants of the virtues spanning so many centuries' by commemorating 'The noble ... Tynicki ... and Druzanna born Kochanowska; the grandson Bernard Tynicki and Bogumiła from Piaseczno; and great-grandson Mikołaj and Anna from Lezen and Petrassi ... and Piotr Tynicki; of the warrior and ancient family of Lastrz, lieutenant of Sandomierz, who remained faithful to God, had been just to his fellow-men, loved his country and was loyal to kings Stefan I and Zygmunt III and died aged seventy-eight.'

In his study *Studenci Polacy na Universytecie Bolońskim w XVI i XVII Wieku* [Polish Students at the University of Bologna in the Sixteenth and Seventeenth Centuries] Mathias Bersohn notes that the scholarly Jerzy Zygmunt Tynicki possessed a formidable library and that Stanisław Tynicki was a leader of the Polish students at Bologna, but concludes tartly that 'The Tynicki family had not distinguished itself in any remarkable way and is little known in the nation's history', despite, apparently, its 'very ornate coat-of-arms'.

In the last years before the war my parents are leading a vigorous social life in Warsaw, with visits to the opera, cabaret and theatre: they attend presidential balls and receptions. They travel abroad on government and business trips and once they take my sister to Vienna, the centre of surgical skills, for yet another operation to adjust her congenitally dislocated hips. She spends long periods immobilised in plaster, and to ease her boredom and discomfort, father has just brought her from Berlin an electric train manufactured by the famous firm of Märklin. It is a large-scale model, satisfyingly solid and heavy and beautifully finished in every detail. Jealous and resentful, I marvel how such a product of intricate engineering can be squandered on a girl who already enjoys a set of remote-controlled racing cars. I console myself with an album of the Great War, full of pictures of strange headless tanks. We also acquire a film-projector which screens Chaplin comedies and newsreels of the Great War. There is amusement all round when I describe the exploding shells as 'thunderstorms from below' and bursting into tears I run out of the darkened room in terror.

I am equally terrified by a noisy circus and an austere incense-saturated procession in St Barbara's, but I enjoy a trip across the Vistula to the zoo in the company of my tall, severe and mustachioed grandfather, Adolf Tynicki, who has arrived on a periodic visit from Dubno, a town near the Soviet border, where he had settled after losing his Ukrainian estate to the Russians. He had married grandmother Paulina after grandmother Franciszka had drowned herself in the middle of the night in a pond on the estate. She was buried in unconsecrated ground. Dim but cherished memories of that gentle, possibly ineffectual woman, who had found it difficult to control two unruly sons, uncles Konstanty and Mieczysław, as well as looking after two daughters, mother and aunt Janka, and who had to endure the autocratic patriarchal manner of her husband, were to haunt my mother always: 'I remember the peaceful little room – three small windows and on wide sills bushy red and rusty begonias in large pots. A spacious sofa stood against the window; the silence broken by the ticking of a large clock. An old bulging chest which was rarely opened, hiding many secrets, and above it a mirror in a mahogany frame which is most vivid in my memory: in it I would see a reflection of myself held in my mother's arms. It was evening. We had all gathered to inspect the lamp father had brought from Berdyczów. And when we were gazing at the lamp a maid knocked on the door and said: "The mistress has been out a long time and she never goes out alone into the garden." '

Grandmother Franciszka's sister, aunt Rozalia Makowska, was deported to Siberia and occasionally news of her reached mother's family.

My own random memories include vanilla ice-cream sold by street vendors; playing with a new toy between the legs of numerous smartly dressed guests at my mother's birthday party; being fooled at Christmas into drinking 'goose-wine' which turned out to be plain water; pocketing some coins of uncle Konstanty's when they slipped out of his black trousers as he was having his afternoon nap with his feet perched high over the bedstead; running to my sister for a cuddle early in the morning after a bad dream in which I spin in a chair round a black hole; rubbing my eyes until I experience a dizzy kaleidoscope; spinning round the room until the room spins round me and I feel sick; watching a military parade (or was it a state funeral?) from a balcony in someone's flat; urged on by my cousin Jacek, shutting myself in the bathroom and spraying the locksmith with water from a hand-held shower when he eventually undoes the door; pointing to nanny when asked who my mother is; admiring my uncle Kazimierz Świtalski's little light-brown Opel car with its recessed chromium door handles, especially when a tiny red light flashed on the dashboard; being made to stand in the corner of our austere black-furnished dining room for refusing to eat peas; watching cook managing the coal-fired stove; being puzzled by the incomprehensible chatter of Zosia's French teacher; joining Jacek in playing a gramophone outside her door to drown the offensive gibberish and complaining to grandpa Tynicki about her; being fascinated by nanny Myszka's severe steel-rimmed glasses that matched her tightly gathered silver hair; climbing onto the terraced roof of the Jabłkowski department store; mounting a children's slide near the parapet and being frozen with fear at the sudden sight of the street way down below; promised to be shown stars in daylight I am instructed to wrap my head in a pyjama jacket and peer at the sky through the sleeve – down which Jacek promptly pours a glass of cold water.

Apparently, my first recorded, grammatically well-formed and factually correct observation was: 'Cows have tails'.

MOTHER REMEMBERS: The Germans are about to attack Poland. The nights are beautiful, moonlit, the crickets are chirping, there is a strange expectation of danger.

COL. WACŁAW LIPINSKI (Propaganda Chief during the defence of Warsaw) records: The last days of August were brimming with an atmosphere of self-confidence and optimism, and the news of the Nazi-Soviet Pact came like lightning from a clear sky. I rushed with this news to Kazimierz Świtalski with whom we had spent hours in the last few months discussing the situation, considering various eventualities.

CHAPTER 2

War

(My view and some other views)

Suddenly the big brown radio in the drawing room is full of agitated voices and strips of ugly brown paper stuck in patterns begin to disfigure the window panes. If there is an air raid, will Zosia reach the shelter in time? After seven operations and many months in plaster, the surgeons had managed to adjust one of her hips, so she now limps and needs a walking-stick.

Suddenly, in the middle of the night we pile into a roomy Chevrolet smelling deliciously of leather and petrol and I wake up in a country house full of suitcases, boxes, bundles and lots of strange people. There are small black aeroplanes with black-and-white crosses flying very low.

This is not Miszewo, the country house north of Warsaw near Płock where we used to spend our summer holidays. That one had red brick walls, was spacious, had parkland at the back overlooked by a verandah. There were stables where Zosia would disappear to play with the horses and the grooms, whom she would incite against the landowning classes, and cause panic among the guests with her revolutionary diatribes. Somewhere at the edge of the park there was a wood with a railway track leading mysteriously into the gloom, probably into a brickworks in a clearing. The house would be full of vacationing Varsovians, but father preferred to spend the hot months in the capital, never shedding his three-piece suit. In the summer of 1938 he returned to take mother and Zosia and the dog on a tour of Poland. My last vivid memory of Miszewo is of the limousine speeding away round the front drive, raising clouds of dust which choked me as I ran after it, crying bitterly at being left behind, having been judged too young to benefit from the experience.

Now I am again bundled into a car in the middle of the night. We drive south-east along refugee-crowded roads and hit a stray pig which explodes like a burst tyre. From time to time the car stops and we rush out to hide in the fields from the bombers roaring overhead. I am still in my pyjamas and deeply embarrassed at being thus exposed to public gaze.

We arrive in Lublin. In the doorway of a house a woman is peeling potatoes into a chamber pot which she promptly empties and hands over to me when she learns of my urgent need. The following day Lublin will be devastated in one of the severest air raids of the campaign. Amongst its many victims will be Józef Czechowicz, one of the leading poets of the time and translator of T. S. Eliot. Some twenty years later a Warsaw weekly will, fortuitously, publish my poems alongside his.

1 SEPTEMBER. ANTHONY DREXEL-BIDDLE JR. US Ambassador to Poland: I awakened at 5.30 in the morning. At first I did not understand what had disturbed me. I went to the window and peered over a tranquil city. All was quiet – and yet I felt trouble was in the air.

STANISŁAW SCHIMITZEK, Administrative Director, Polish Foreign Ministry: In the main hall [of the Foreign Ministry] in an appropriately visible place Jadwiga Beckowa [wife of Józef Beck, the Foreign Minister] worked at a specially installed telephone, taking turns with her 'ladies-in-waiting' at an anti-aircraft monitoring post, gathering information about bombing raids broadcast by radio.

Foreign Minister JÓZEF BECK to COUNT EDWARD RACZYŃSKI, Polish Ambassador at the Court of St James: The Polish Government expresses the conviction that in accordance with existing treaties it will receive immediate support from its allies.

LEON NOËL, French Ambassador to Poland: The moment German aggression began, Poland began to demand from its allies the support they had undertaken to provide, particularly the immediate deployment of their air forces in battle. But neither the British nor the French Government was ready for this.

2 SEPTEMBER. JAN WŁODZIMIERZ JÓZEF CEZARY STANISŁAW PIOTR KLEMENS ZYGMUNT SZEMBEK, First Under-Secretary at the Foreign Ministry: During lunch at Mr and Mrs Beck's, which I attended, the Minister emphasised the excellent morale of our troops, the heroic stand of our Westerplatte garrison, the sizeable number of German aircraft shot down, etc. The assembled company were impatiently awaiting news from London and Paris regarding the entry of Britain and France into the war on our side. Princess Radziwiłł, who arrived in Warsaw to help with the organisation of the hospitals, was expressing her anger at the recalcitrance and irresponsibility of the British. She said that General

Carton de Wiart [the British military attaché] was clearly impatient and was apparently considering resigning: in the city great anger is turned against the British.

3 SEPTEMBER. SZEMBEK: The news of Britain declaring war on Germany spread throughout the Ministry with great enthusiasm. There was a general conviction that this was a turning point and that the British would now start bombing German cities. The sounds of joyful demonstrators were rising from the streets. I had lunch with Mr and Mrs Beck. Mrs Beck placed a British flag on the table. People spoke as if German defeat was a matter of a short time. The Minister said: 'How fortunate I signed a treaty with Britain and that on my return from London I did not engage in any rotten discussions with the Germans. We might have had the war postponed, but then would have had it in the spring, and we would have had to fight it alone.'

SCHIMITZEK: Despite the danger of an air raid at any moment crowds from all parts of Warsaw converged on the British embassy. Beck had to push his way into the embassy through the joyful crowds.

4 SEPTEMBER. SCHIMITZEK: The first major air raid. Dark clouds of smoke rose above the city and buildings were bursting into flames.

COL. LIPIŃSKI: News from the front not good. The Germans announce they have taken Bydgoszcz and Grudziądz and – which sounds improbable but must be true – that they have also taken Kraków. But the general news is better. Churchill and Eden have entered the British Government. This means a fight to the finish, fierce and unconditional.

5 SEPTEMBER. Minister **BECK:** Premier Składkowski informed me of the decision to move the Government to the Wołyń District [in Eastern Poland], with its centre in Łuck but with the Foreign Ministry and the diplomatic corps intended first for Włodzimierz and then for Krzemieniec.

6 SEPTEMBER. COL. LIPIŃSKI: Thousands are continuing to leave the capital. The evacuation of the Government, carried out with such improper haste, has created in Warsaw a mood of panic which is spreading like a disease. All those who have public duties are rushing beyond the Vistula, driven by fear and terror. Only a few days ago everybody was so heroic, full of the will to fight and see it through. A handful of bombs, a few explosions, the proximity of the Germans, have turned these people into a cowardly mob. Returning home I present the case clearly: Warsaw will fight, leaving it is senseless, I am staying behind.

7 SEPTEMBER. BIDDLE: Dry weather had made the roads exceedingly dusty – a white pulverised dust arose in the wake of each car like a thick fog, and frequently took three to four minutes to settle sufficiently to permit visibility. One frequently passed lengthy lines of troop-laden buses and lorries, and columns of mechanised equipment, including artillery of various calibre. This, the lack of light, the narrowness of the average road, and the exasperating dust contributed towards making the driver's task an uncomfortable one. [The German] pilots became increasingly daring in their general operations, power-diving to surprisingly low altitudes and frequently 'hawking' traffic along the highways. After refuelling in Łuck, each car of our Embassy group in turn proceeded through Dubno to Krzemieniec. At the outskirts of Dubno ... we stopped under some trees during an aerial bombardment of the railway yards.

10 SEPTEMBER. NOËL: In Krzemieniec the local population was expecting the swift arrival of the Soviet army. There were rumours in circulation about an agreement reached between Berlin and Moscow concerning a partition of Poland. The very numerous Jews in these parts were awaiting the Red Army with undisguised impatience. Some Ukrainians were placing their hopes in Hitler, others in Stalin.

12 SEPTEMBER. NOËL (in Krzemieniec): It was clear that unless the allied armies begin their offensive action in the west as a matter of urgency, the eastern front will cease to exist and all hopes of forcing the Germans to fight on two fronts will evaporate. The French Government and the Supreme Command, which were kept up to date on the situation by General Musse's and my reports, were aware of this. However, our appeals remained unanswered. I had not realised the extent to which our army was incapable of any action whatsoever.

13 SEPTEMBER. BIDDLE: Paris and London official circles were informing the Polish Ambassadors in both capitals that they hesitated to permit their respective air forces to bombard German communications and war industrial plants, for fear of the potential unfavourable effect thereof on American public opinion. Minister Beck stated that he had already participated in two wars: the Great War and the Polish War with the Bolsheviks [in 1920]. In this third war he had had to stand aside. However, he still hoped to take active part in the fourth war, and perhaps to end his days on a battlefield as had

his forefathers. I gained the impression that the Minister was suffering from deep emotions and mixed feelings about the performance of Poland's military establishment. In fact, I felt he knew at that time that nothing could really pull the chestnuts out of the fire for Poland.

14 SEPTEMBER. SCHIMITZEK: The diplomatic corps, evacuated to Zaleszczyki, is to be gathered in Kosów and housed in the buildings of Dr Apolinary Tarnawski's sanatorium.

SZEMBEK: Kosowo is full of officer-pilots who are to be transported to France via Romania.

15 SEPTEMBER. SZEMBEK (ZALESZCZYKI-KUTY): We reviewed our policies and searched for those mistakes that could have caused the present catastrophe. The policy assumptions were undoubtedly correct but we conducted a big-power policy without being a big power.

16 SEPTEMBER. STANISŁAW ZABIEŁŁO (Foreign Ministry official): Minister Archiszewski told me that the matter of our transit passage through Romania to France is in principle settled. It was a beautiful summer-like day.

COL. LIPIŃSKI (WARSAW): Fires in the city centre from bombs and incendiary grenades, huge fires in Praga and Grochów. Along the Aleje and Nowy Świat half in the darkness of the night, half illuminated by the fire glare, columns march east. In the silence all you could hear was the slow hoofbeat of hundreds of horses pulling carts, artillery and equipment.

17 SEPTEMBER. NOËL (KUTY): We learnt at 7 a.m. that

Soviet troops had entered Poland at dawn along the whole frontier. In these regions totally denuded of [Polish] units their advance was very swift.

COL. LIPINSKI: On return from Command Headquarters I receive terrible, frightening news on the radio. The Bolsheviks have crossed the frontier. It was clear that something had been brewing but I was deluding myself into thinking that they wouldn't dare, that it wouldn't happen so swiftly.

MOTHER REMEMBERS: Fleeing from Warsaw to Dłużewo near Mińsk. The manor house with the coat-of-arms on the outside, while inside it's bedlam! The Germans bomb us. After a couple of days we flee east to Lublin, then Krasnystaw, which they bomb terribly and we rush out of the train several times into the fields. My heart against the earth pounding strongly. Through the night we travel through Kowel to Dubno, the night is long and dark, the carriages dirty. We arrive in Dubno, the autumn is beautifully golden. Here we meet chaos and gloom. They are bombing again. Naively we thought that bombs would not reach there – fleeing into fields, and hungry days, for no one thinks of food, and terror shakes us constantly. We flee beyond Krzemieniec to Młynowce.

FATHER WRITES: In accordance with the order issued by my commanding officer, I left Poland on 17 September, travelling through Kuty to Romania. I left my family behind in Młynowce, a God-forsaken Ukrainian village, on the estate of the Castellati family, beyond Wiśniowiec near Krzemieniec.

ZOSIA WRITES: Dear Daddy!

Mummy wants me to describe our trek for you, so I am getting down to the job at once.

I wanted to cry terribly when you left us in Młynowce. On Sunday, 17 September we left in a cart for Wiśniowiec. The ride was extraordinary, it rained cats and dogs and we sat there all covered up, like mounds of misery. We lodged in a terrible hole belonging to a Jew called Margolis. The Jews were quite good to us. Mummy and I slept on the floor. The priest's house-keeper cooked our dinners. There was nowhere to wash and vermin crawled over us at night.

Every day we expected the Bolsheviks to arrive. They came on 22 September.

18 SEPTEMBER. LUIS DE PEDROSO, The Spanish Ambassador to Poland (ČERNOVCY, ROMANIA): The Polish Government in its entirety has been interned in Romania.

DREXEL BIDDLE (ČERNOVCY): During the course of the day Polish Government circles learnt that under threat of aggression Berlin had forbidden Bucharest to allow safe transit of the Polish government through Romania.

PEDROSO: Throughout the night of the 17th and also during the 18th and 19th an unending stream of cars, in which thousands of Poles escaped from their native land to Romania, was passing through Černovcy. I have never before witnessed such a sad spectacle, nor have I ever seen people more depressed. However, none of them had lost faith in the future of Poland, whatever its present state. One gets the impression that all those virtues of their ancestors, who had many times witnessed the death throes of this great nation, were being reborn in the present generation.

Further east, in Dubno, we find lodgings in a house and say goodbye to father, whose army unit is stationed nearby. My grandparents have a house on the outskirts and we spend our days sheltering from air raids in a potato field and then we learn that the Russians are coming. A civilian goes from door to door issuing mandatory invitations to agit-prop meetings and distributing portraits of Stalin. He instructs mother to display him in a window suitably embellished. Mother, a teenage witness of the glories of the Russian Revolution, knows exactly how to respond. She presses the picture passionately to her bosom and eagerly promises to honour the Leader of Nations. There follows a frantic search for suitable drapes. The Father of Mankind eventually appears in the window resting in the folds of mother's vivid red blouse (with the cut-glass buttons discreetly tucked away) and supported on a bunch of red-skinned sausages. The dark-panelled room with a low ceiling now appears even darker but mother derives much-needed cheer from this little comic turn and the giggles of passers-by give us satisfaction. Her ability to respond in a spirit of levity and humour will serve her well in the grim months and years ahead.

Through the windows we now watch wide columns of Polish soldiers marching guarded by armed Soviet troops walking at intervals alongside. We try to spot father. That night mother decides we should start retreating west and leave Rozetka with our grandparents. It's pitch dark when we pile into a horse-drawn carriage. Mother is still at the door saying goodbye and we can hear the dog whining and whimpering. Suddenly the complaining stops and the characteristic tinkle of the dog's registration medallion striking the collar can be heard nearer and nearer. Zosia is beside herself with joy at mother's last-minute change of mind. But my most vivid memory of Dubno is the flavour of grandfather's honey from his beehives.

We now spend days and nights queuing for space on battered Pullman trains and bulging buses. A man on a bus holding a jar of precious pig's lard is not pleased when he discovers it's been licked away by Rozetka as she leans skilfully over mother's shoulder. Another passenger, also a refugee from Warsaw, borrows a coat from us which he promises to return in Warsaw.

23 SEPTEMBER. SZEMBEK (Paris:) No action took place on the part of the allied powers to free members of our Government [interned in Romania]. The freeing of the President is important to the extent that, after the fall of Warsaw, which may happen at any moment, the Germans might organise some fictitious government in Poland and this would compromise our international situation completely.

FATHER REPORTS: While being transported to an internment camp in Tulcza, I managed to escape to Bucharest. I immediately undertook to get my family out of Poland with the help of smugglers. The chances looked good because my family was in south-eastern Poland from where such actions had already proved successful. When this attempt failed [because father was unable to establish contact with us] I sought visas for them to Romania, documents which many Polish citizens had acquired, but this route too proved closed to me because I lacked the 30,000 or so lei for the various fees. In the end I was helped in getting these visas by Minister Beck through his personal intervention with the Romanian Foreign Minister, Gafencu. But I could not make use of them because of the difficulties which the

Germans had meanwhile imposed upon the Romanians to oppose any help for the Poles.

25 SEPTEMBER. COL. LIPIŃSKI (Warsaw): The whistling of bombs never stops, explosions hit all around continually. The sky covered in smoke, the repetitive roar of diving aeroplanes. I am beginning to feel somewhat lonely in the emptiness of this city which is being murdered. My only companion is my Opel. Driving through the centre I didn't see a single human being. The sun is warm and clear, but through the smoke from fires which have now engulfed the whole capital, I can only see the sun's bloody disc as though during some terrible natural cataclysm.

I try to walk through to the Jewish quarter because there apparently the destruction and the fires are most intense. I walk a few hundred yards and have to retreat. There is no way through because not only are buildings on fire on both sides but burning walls are beginning to fall onto the street. The scene is unbearable, and even my steady nerves give up: I feel defeated. People are running through the burning streets. They are screaming wildly, they clutch bundles and suitcases, the desperate sobbing of little defenceless children. These people are running from building to building, only to be driven out from each in turn by the leaping flames. At that moment, somewhere between Wielka Street and Grzybowska Street I reached a decision – enough. We have no right. Warsaw has done its share – the time to end it all has come.

26 SEPTEMBER. ZABIELLO (Paris): In a country [Romania] where at that time bribes meant everything and the authorities demonstrated a remarkable incompetence, unless they had their own interest to safeguard, after a year almost all the top brass of the regime were able to escape. Only Beck was guarded right to the end.

28 SEPTEMBER. ZABIEŁŁO (Paris): Beck, who towered above the remaining members of the Government and had imposd his will on them, probably realised very quickly that departure from Romania was a lost cause. Between Slanic [where Beck was interned] and the President's residence at Bicaz, Beck's emissaries shuttled continuously – usually one or other of the Drymmer couple [Drymmer was a high level Foreign Ministry official, his wife was my godmother]. After the trauma of September Beck was in a very poor state and was almost always ill, eaten away by tuberculosis which overwhelmed him a couple of years later. [He died in 1944].

Some other isolated memories: we rush for a train on a blackened station, I fall and my nose bleeds profusely. I lose my newly acquired cardboard setsquare in the deep black mud of the marketplace in Wiśniowiec and on a nearby farm I work my way through a bucketful of newly picked pears, while mother chats to the farmer. The succeeding tummy ache is excruciating but the taste of those pears remains unforgettable; decades later in a moment of revelation in a Yorkshire country house I rediscover the scent of fruit stored on a stone floor. One night we shelter with a Jewish family in a house on a cobbled street in Włodzimierz: by the light of a candle, Zosia starts teaching me to read from an oblong primer wrapped in oily red paper. The host marvels at my progress and predicts, 'He'll end up Prime Minister'. Back in Warsaw grandmother

Czerniawska had already predicted I would be a bishop and had thoughtfully insisted on my being baptised 'Adam' in honour of Cardinal Adam Sapieha. I stay awake all night because a child screams in pain from a septic finger.

At a railway station there are locked goods wagons in the sidings and through tiny chinks men are calling out for matches and cigarettes. These are the first batches of Polish deportees to the Soviet Union. Eventually over a million men, women and young children will end up in Soviet labour camps. Those still alive in 1941 will be allowed by Stalin to make their way out of the Soviet Union. I shall come across them in the Middle East.

We are now huddled in a corner of the station hall, which is full of Russian soldiers who are taking an increasing interest in us and teasing the dog. They compliment mother on caring for granny in such times, but mother is becoming increasingly nervous in case grumpy old Myszka should say something to betray her status as nanny in a bourgeois household. Suspicious-looking Polish-speaking civilians are also hovering nearby. Just then I beg mother to ask one of the soldiers to give me the red star he has pinned to his forage cap. She is relieved at being able to promote this unexpected diversionary gesture of goodwill, while as for me, I am still too innocent to feel guilty at handling the emblem of Soviet domination.

ZOSIA REPORTS: Finally the Jews had had enough of us, so on 24 September we moved to Nowy Wiśniowiec. We lodged with a pock-marked hag who at once started lecturing us that the war is due to the ladies in Warsaw being immoral and smoking cigarettes. She herself was so terribly proper that she sold us apples at twice the price.

We had two rooms and a kitchen and we slept as never before. Adam slept on a sack of straw on a board supported on two stools, and he didn't even know it until he saw it all in the morning. Next to the board was a settee hard as a stone and as narrow as spaghetti. This distinguished bed was occupied by Panna Władysława. Mummy, Rozunia and I slept in the most interesting bed: it was made up of four poles and a sack. As if this wasn't enough, the old hag gave Adam, Burek and Janusz clay horses on which they whistled constantly. The noise was awful.

On 1 October, a Sunday, we caught a terribly crowded bus for Krzemieniec.

MOTHER REMEMBERS: When the bus finally arrived after several hours I was shocked to realise there wasn't space for us. Suddenly a man appeared and with triumphant determination pushed the four of us with the dog and our bundles inside. He wished us a good journey and called out in Ukrainian: 'You'll always remember the man from Wiśniowiec who was so good to you!'

ZOSIA REPORTS: In Krzemieniec we spent the night in one room with five gentlemen. At seven in the morning we were waiting for a train to Dubno. It wasn't till seven at night that we arrived in Dubno travelling in a manure-covered cattle truck. We spent the night on the floor in the station. In the morning a cart took us to Suromicze [mother's parents' house on the outskirts of Dubno]. Our dear family wasn't that happy to see us. We were very pleased with the money you [i.e. father] left us with [the chemist] Mr Kozakiewicz [whom we were to meet again in 1942, in Palestine where he arrived after being released from a Soviet labour camp]. On 11 October we moved to Dubno.

MOTHER REMEMBERS: We lodged next to the NKVD [the Soviet Secret Police]. They were marching our soldiers, prisoners-of-war. Each one had a different cap, representing the various regiments. My heart bled seeing these emaciated wretches being marched past every morning. And then came the order to decorate our windows red for Stalin's anniversary. I had no money to buy decorations; my red blouse saved us and so his august visage looked out from our window in the embrace of my blouse. The irony of fate: one never knows what will come in useful.

Depressed, I fell into a state of apathy and lethargy. It was October and every evening I went to church where I relaxed in the semi-darkness, staring at the candles round the statue of the Madonna.

ZOSIA REPORTS: I was terribly bored in Dubno. The day would begin early. Mother would get up at dawn and go to the market to trade with the women in the market place. Panna Władysława threw tantrums pretending she wasn't being allowed to stand in queues or go to market. Whenever she finally got round to going, the women would long ago have disappeared behind their stoves at home. So mummy would always go and always there were rows. When one lady, who had the reputation of being the greatest musician in Dubno, once gave a recital on her shaking wreck of a piano, the sparrows on the roof woke up and the mice ran away into their holes. Altogether life like a witch's in hell.

One day uncle Kocio arrived and advised us to go to Lwów. We agreed and at night we took a cab to the station. We stopped at Suromicze, where we were to leave Rozunia. I was crying when I handed her to mummy who took her to grandpa. After a while I heard mummy's footsteps and suddenly I heard something like the sound of the registration tag attached to her lead. And I wasn't wrong – mummy was coming back with her. Rozunia all muddy jumped on my knees squealing with joy. What had happened: when mummy had handed the lead to granny, Rozunia had begun to squeal and mother did not have the heart to leave her. We reached the station. There was no chance of boarding the train, not even of squeezing onto the station. So we returned to Dubno and decided to go to Łuck in the morning by bus.

At eight in the morning we were at the station and waited all day. At last, in the evening they said nothing doing until tomorrow morning. So again we went back and the next day at the same time we were at the station and half an hour later we were sitting in the bus. Grandpa was crying when he said goodbye. [That was the last time we saw him]. Under the pressure of war my grandparents will drift westwards, eventually settling and dying in Tarnów. There the Czerniawski family vault was ready to receive them.

On the way we and the bus nearly somersaulted into a ditch. At ten we were in Łuck. We had breakfast and lunch and spent the rest of the time in the street in mud on top of a mound of bundles. Evening began to fall. Luckily a driver turned up who accepted a bribe to let us sleep in a bus which was leaving for Włodzimierz in the morning. When it was totally dark we all squashed into the dark bus where they locked us up like herring in a barrel. Everybody was dead-beat and irritable and in the darkness you could hear people nervously biting sunflower seeds, murmuring and yawning. I snuggled into a corner and fell asleep with difficulty and when I woke I had the feeling I had been used as a corkscrew.

At seven in the morning we left and at nine were in the famous city of Włodzimierz. We were to leave at once for Uściług but the [new German-Soviet] border was closed. We got out in search of a toilet. We found one of a kind I'm sure you've never seen in your life. You had to climb to the first floor and despite all efforts you could easily fall out of it and kill yourself [because it had no back wall]. This toilet was jealously secured with a padlock.

MOTHER REMEMBERS: In Włodzimierz I slept with the children in a connecting room and all the time groups of refugees with their bundles traipsed to their sleeping-cells further on. Someone with an ulcer moaned throughout the night. Adaś sat quietly in the corner of the room, moving his finger over a newspaper. Noticing Adaś reading, and he was only four, our very sympathetic Jewish host was visibly fascinated. 'You'll see,' he said to me, 'One day he will be a minister.' 'God forbid!' I cried. 'Can't you see what's happened to all our ministers?!'

ZOSIA REPORTS: They wouldn't open the border while we waited so we went back to Łuck. There we immediately took a cab to the [railway] station. The station was overflowing with refugees. God! How we suffered in that stuffy station! Panna W. managed to secure a space and two chairs for Adam and made a bed out of them for him and wouldn't let anyone push against him. The train arrived after some twelve hours.

We emerged onto the platform. Heavy rain was falling, people were crowding into the train. Eventually we too managed to push our way in. Panna Władysława was screaming that no one was helping her. People couldn't stand that and cried 'Shut up you hysterical hag!' She cowered and murmured furiously.

MOTHER REMEMBERS: We travelled a long time in an unlit compartment, it was very cold and dirty. In Lwów I spent an hour looking for Konstanty: the address I had was unclear. What I once experienced in a dream: walking endlessly, never finding the goal of the journey. It was late at night that we had dinner with Pan and Pani Zaleski, later deported to the Soviet Union. Then a bath in which I drowned the lice.

ZOSIA REPORTS: At nine we arrived in Lwów. We had a room let by Pani Krasuska who was very good to us and has come with us [to Warsaw]. Adaś has learnt to read. The following day I had a bath. So days came and went.

In Lwów mother is interrogated and, unlike other officers' wives who boast of their status, demanding proper treatment, and are therefore promptly led away, she confesses to being the wife of a mechanic lost somewhere in the turmoils of war, and hopes her furs turned inside out will not betray her. Her fluent Russian and her ability to use the appropriate agit-prop patter ensures her safe-conduct. The Russians in a confident mood are ready to march on Buckingham Palace – that 'toothless old hag' – and they are not daunted by Polish women addressing them as 'heroes with nipples on their heads' on account of their strangely shaped hats. Comic relief is also provided by three Russian officers who lodge with the same landlady as we do. Two are needed to help a third wash himself: one flushes the water, the other uses his hands to dam the water in the basin. People are told to register with the authorities if they want to go back west, but someone says it is a ruse by the Russians to prepare lists of those to be deported east into the Soviet Union. Someone else sees the present events as a fulfilment of an ancient prophecy that the black eagle and the falcon will feast on the flesh of a cock.

CHAPTER 3

The Nine-day Wander

3–11 December 1939

Mother is now convinced that the Germans will be the lesser evil, and with some other refugees makes contact with guides who are willing to take us through forests back to the German side. But the guides are not keen on a party which includes a yapping dog and a crippled teenager. Additional rewards in the form of tinned food, clothing and jewellery and assurance that the dog understands the gravity of the situation, finally persuade the men and they lead us into a calm silver night. Before reaching the forests we have to cross some open country with a scattering of trees and bushes. Just then a Soviet lorry is seen approaching head on. There is no time to run. We all freeze behind some bushes and the lorry, full of merry men, bumps on past us along the track.

We spend several days marching along paths through dense forests. The alarm is raised when loud voices and strange metallic sounds are heard ahead. These are discovered to emanate from just one individual, known to our guides, who had bought a large saw in the market. He was striking the trees as he passed in accompaniment to his inebriated song. Rozetka retains her self-control and Zosia limps along bravely but the guides have to carry her from time to time. We approach the border on the river in the dead of night. It is pitch dark and very cold. We wade across and reach a cottage on the other side. I ride piggy-back on the shoulders of one of the guides but he stumbles and drops me into the icy waters. They fish me out and there is a terrible stillness as everyone strains to hear whether the border guards have heard anything. Fortunately, there is no sound and we are soon warming ourselves by an iron stove in a cottage which, oddly enough, belongs to a friendly German settler family. In the morning I stumble against the iron stove and blood gushes profusely from my forehead. Soon we have to leave and as I ride on a cart in a bundle of straw with only my bandaged head showing, German patrols, on the look-out for stray Polish soldiers, observe me closely.

MOTHER REMEMBERS: From Lwów we started in the direction of the new German-Soviet border in the company of Pani Krasuska, her brother and her son. We walk through a forest, the moon is bright and full, beyond the pines Soviet lorries appear, in fear of arrest we knock at the door of a hut. We are refused shelter by the people who fear punishment for harbouring refugees. Adaś can't walk any further, he keeps collapsing, Zosia too . . .

ZOSIA REPORTS: On 3 December we set out with Pani Krasuska, her son and her brother. We were assisted by a certain Pan Fin whom Pani Krasuska called Dziunek. We were taken on a flat cart to the station and went by train to Surochow. At Surochow we got out [because the line into German-occupied Poland was cut]: it was so dark you couldn't see your own fingers. Adam fell flat on his face and blood was gushing from his nose. In the end we got into a cart, mercifully with a covering because the rain was heavy. Just think, Daddy, 28 kilometres in deep mud in the rain. We covered ourselves with an eiderdown but we were still cold. After nine hours we reached Sieniawa.

In the morning we marched 3.5 kilometres to a cottage in the village of Wylewy. There we slept in dirty beds till noon. Then we again went to bed at night. Voices woke me: it was the guides arguing with Pani Krasuska's brother, steadily raising the fee which was finally settled at 600 złoty.

Everybody went on foot, except that I, Panna W., Adam and a boy who helped with luggage, went in a cart. We got off the road, leaping over streams and ditches. Eventually we drove through a pond and nearly fell off the cart. That was when I saw the moon rising for the first time. Eventually a light appeared in a window among trees and after a while we stopped outside a cottage. I entered the room which measured three by four metres and half of it contained a huge stove. An old hag sat on top of the stove and she screeched constantly. On straw against the wall a woman slept with her child. On a bench sat people who had just crossed the border [presumably from the German to the Russian side]. All in all, there were probably twenty people there and all of them milling around. Then they started arguing that they wanted cash in hand, but we wouldn't agree because we didn't know what type of people they were, and they were supposed to receive the money from Pan F. after we had crossed the border [to the German side]. The row went on for about an hour.

That night in a cart through fields, and fording ponds and streams, we arrived at the cottage of a scoundrel who, instead of guiding us on, stole from us.

Dearest Daddy!

I am writing this letter on 18 February [1940]. It's the fifth with an account of our adventures.

When at last, after a long argument, the peasants agreed to guide us, Adam kept falling down, he was so sleepy. Finally, we move off. It's a beautiful, moonlit night, it's as light as day. It's turned frosty. The ground squeaks loudly underfoot. People advise against the march but Pani Krasuska insists. The guides rush ahead madly. Men groan under Pani Krasuska's bundles. And suddenly we hear a loud crash bang! One of the men had dropped a suitcase and he's holding only the handle which broke off. He stands there helpless with a sheepish look. Another nearly fell over. You can imagine how quietly we marched, just like a herd of elephants. We enter a small thicket which looks very mysterious and very beautiful. Suddenly Pan Józef, Pani Irena Krasuska's brother, catches up with us. He is very worried and asks whether Pani Irka is with us. Only then we notice she isn't. Pan Józef turns back, looks everywhere, but Pani Irka had vanished together with her son like a stone dropped in the water. We decide not to go further, we spend the night in a cottage which was supposed to be nearby but turned out to be quite a long way off. It wasn't until six in the morning that we found Pani Irka.

That evening we returned to Sieniawa in a cart. We spent a long time plopping through the mud. Rozunia was all wet and so tired she wanted to lie down immediately. We spent the morning selling our things. It was only then we noticed our bundle was stolen but there was nothing we could do. In the evening we were just about to go to bed when suddenly a restaurateur we knew found for us decent men who undertook to guide us for a smaller fee. We packed and off we went. We passed quietly through the sleeping town and entered a field. On the way Pan Józef fell into a watery ditch with his luggage. We walked seven kilometres across fields, meadows, ditches and my feet kept sliding about in the mud, like a cow's on ice.

MOTHER ADDS: Don't you think Zosia is good at describing? Perhaps fate will compensate her for her disability and will grant her gifts in this direction.

MOTHER REMEMBERS: A guide carried Zosia piggy-back because the poor child couldn't walk on account of her operations; nanny led Adaś by the hand, Rozetka ran alongside with her number-tag ringing gently and the guides insisted it should be taken off. Then suddenly we hear a different metallic sound. The guides dropped the bundles and we scattered through the dark wood. Suddenly we see a solitary man emerging, carrying a large scythe which he bought on the other side of the border. Relieved that this wasn't a Soviet patrol, we began questioning him about the other side, but each time he replied: 'Just so, that's well understood'.

ZOSIA REPORTS: We slept on straw and in the afternoon we were on the move. We walked through beautiful forests, then on planks across dams, past a large lake called Goplana. Then we pushed our way through bushes which scratched us mightily. We finally reached a forest track, when suddenly we heard the sound of steel. Everyone in panic scattered into the trees, dropping the luggage on the way. It turned out it was a peasant carrying a saw which made this ringing sound. We took this man on to carry the luggage.

We moved on. Pan Józef carried me piggy-back and the poor chap had quite a struggle. At last we emerged from the forest onto a large clearing. Everyone began running, I was falling behind and I got frightened I wouldn't be able to keep up. But, thank God, the river was just in front of us. People began jumping into the water, I could hear the loud splash! Splash! Just beyond the river there was a ditch filled with water, the man carrying Adam fell into the water but only Adam's feet got wet. Later Adam confided in me that he thought he would drown. I lost my patience waiting, so I started lowering myself into the water, but I fell into the same hole that Adam did. I dragged myself some four kilometres to the cottage. I lay on the straw and slept dead to the world. I forgot to tell you that the one with the saw stole Pani Krasuska's baggage, but the people found him and got 100 złoty reward.

The next day we were taken in a cart to the river San and crossed it on a ferry together with the cart. After seven hours we arrived in Leżajsk which was only seventeen kilometres away. There we met two ladies who told us the ferrymen had told them about three children who kept quiet and a dog which didn't bark.

After a night spent in a deserted house where I sleep on a bare table, we eventually reach Kraków. In the Market Square outside St Mary's Church, mother buys me a rosary in a yellow plastic box shaped like a Bible, but I insist on also having a grey-blue devil whose tongue, ears and tail pop out menacingly when I squeeze his belly. We then go in to pray in the candle-lit gothic gloom of St Mary's.

ZOSIA REPORTS: In Kraków we ate lunch at Hawełka's restaurant and Rozetka was next to me eating from an ashtray.

MOTHER ADDS: There were many Germans in uniform, their wives elegantly dressed, while we appeared like a band of tramps.

Then I went to St Mary's Church to pray and to offer thanks to God. There were many Germans kneeling, clearly they were very religious. It was difficult to get seats in a train for Warsaw but in the end I managed with a bribe.

CHAPTER 4

Wir sind in Warshau!

MOTHER REMEMBERS: [We boarded the train with] the Krasuski family, with whom we crossed illegally from the Bolshevik to the German occupation. We boarded a comfortable, roomy train, unfortunately full of Germans, whose uniforms irritate and whose rudeness annoys. It's terrible and hard to believe that we are under the Prussian heel.

The train took a long time. The Gestapo man would often open the door, calling 'Paßsheine bitte'. He eyed our sacks with contempt. On the Soviet side we had to destroy our luggage with its Paris stickers and other embellishments which advertised us as people from a different class and enemies of communism. I filled the sacks with the oddments that remained.

Outside the windows large flakes of snow twist – the first snow. The children are asleep. My legs ache and I can't find a place to rest my head which I have to keep against a jutting partition in the seat.

Warsaw at last, the longed-for Warsaw. At the station I look around fearfully. A grey crowd with bundles on their backs shuffles through the station halls and we follow. There is a silence: there are no taxis or cabs, there are only push-trolleys. I glance surreptitiously up and down Aleje Jerozolimskie and rejoice at seeing the houses standing large and undamaged, but there are crosses on graves in the squares. Snow is falling and it is excruciatingly cold and sad.

I've guarded the key to my flat as something very special. I longed to use it to enter the flat as in the old times. Will it work? The key was long and thin and used to unlock the door smoothly. Great was the shock. I saw an emptiness and many strange faces. On the floor I found a gas mask, a bottle with holy water from Lourdes, and one of my handkerchiefs which I have kept ever since. The rooms, where we lived and enjoyed life, where many good friends enjoyed the warm atmosphere of our company, were empty and without window panes.

The cactuses on the balcony were covered in snow. Under the snow they were green but they collapsed like punctured balloons when the snow was removed.

ZOSIA REPORTS: In the flat we found two lady lodgers in Kocio's room, and in the kitchen and in [cook] Renia's room there was a certain Gdoski couple with their lawyer sonny. Not a single window pane in any of the rooms, everywhere was empty and cold. Your photographs [i.e. father's] lay on the floor so I gathered them all up. In the drawing room, above the door to the dining room, there is a hole from a grenade. Total ruination.

MOTHER REMEMBERS: After the discomforts of our journey it was very pleasant to be back in Warsaw, for that city had, for anyone who had lived there for many years, a special charm and was carefree even though its problems were now immense.

There is a pile of light-brown bomb rubble in the drawing room and a nauseating smell as though a giant had been sick there. Mother's dark portrait, with the eyes shot out, is still hanging on the wall next to the crater. There are squatters occupying some of the other rooms but we manage to carve out a territory for ourselves. Most importantly, Zosia's electric train is safe and I am now allowed to play with it.

It is bitterly cold everywhere. We make forays to find coal and food. Some of the squatters are persuaded to leave. The man who had borrowed the coat from mother in the east now brings it back. This act of ordinary decent normality seems to everyone particularly impressive against a background of universal destruction, chaos and despair. And just before Christmas, mother receives an unexpected present: father sends a card from Bucharest. This is the first indication after three months that he is alive. She responds with a few words on a postcard, written, just in case, in German: *Wir sind in Warshau!*

MOTHER REMEMBERS: A cruel winter set in. I began selling my precious rings to buy food. A student fixed window panes in one of the rooms, we had a stove mounted, and we began to live there, the four of us in one room with the piano.

Ghosts: Zosia reports

[While we were waiting to move into our own flat] we

went to stay in Mrs Białobrzeska's flat. It was so cold it was unbelievable. But it was worst one night when ghosts gave us a fright. One night I was woken up about one o'clock by crackling noises and Panna Władysława calling, 'Can you hear that, Madam?' 'I can', mummy says, and again I can hear trakh! trakh! trakh! Our hair stands on end because we are alone in the flat. But mummy heroically jumped out of bed, turned on the lights, pushed the trunks against the door and began yelling, 'Who is there ?!' Then she returned to bed. After a while we hear Panna Władysława moaning loudly, 'Ooooh! Oooooh!' It turned out Panna W was groaning like this from fear. So mother told her to climb on top of the trunks and look through the glass-panel. At this Panna W squealed 'Ooooh! Oooooh! What if I see some brute there!'

In the morning it transpired it was a basket creaking. The following night someone quite clearly ran past the door. But I think it was a housemaid.

A church service: Zosia reports

This Thursday I went to the chapel in Roma [the cinema next door to our flat] because [St Barbara's] church is in ruins. The chapel isn't that large. It was so packed I was nearly squashed. Instead of praying, people jostle so hard that you get quite a bruising. At last I managed to get out behind a fat lady who felt faint, although this faintness wasn't all that apparent, because she was thrusting her elbows right and left, making people groan. When I finally got out with Renia G (for we were together) we were sweating like mice stuck under a broom. Today we had a super breakfast with ham and sausage. We had guests: Jacek, aunt [Janka] and Pani Stecka.

'Honour and Motherland': Mother recalls

I boarded the tram at Rakowiecka Street. We move slowly, the tram shudders and shakes. I ask the conductor why are we going so slowly. 'The track is war-damaged,' so we go bump bump taking thirty minutes to Warecka Street. People are sitting deep in thought, self-absorbed. There is a barrier inside the tram. The front section is for Germans only. I glance furtively at their section. A German soldier has taken it over, just like the frost on the windows, a terrible powerful freeze which stifles your breathing. The frost has drawn silvery flowers on the tram windows. We seem to be travelling inside an icy tunnel. People often get off in the wrong places because they can't see the tram stops.

We turn the corner in Puławska Street, the rails squeal piercingly. On the corner they've fixed His Master's Voice loudspeakers which scream fiendishly: So many bombs dropped on Coventry! So many on Birmingham! We move into Aleje Ujazdowskie, a beautiful thoroughfare, now like a sad cemetery, because the Belvedere Palace is quiet and mysterious, the Łazienki Park is closed, surrounded by guards, the benches empty, Chopin's statue removed, with only the plinth remaining. On the left, [the pre-war] Polish Army Headquarters.

Ranges of burnt-out buildings, with pane-less staring windows, oozing a grim blackness; the streaks of burning are firmly fixed on these walls, and above them, untouched by the flames, the inscription 'Honour and Motherland'!

Danse Macabre: Mother recalls

The snow white like swan's down, the sun blazes and
sparkles, hurting the eyes. I walk fast because there is a
terrible frost. The snow has in places covered up the
war damage. I walk faster and faster spurred on by the
growing cold; it's difficult to breathe, while the boots
and the heavy clothes impede rapid movement, and
you have to be quick because the curfew, the nightmare
of all the citizens, is fast approaching. Often we have to
break into a jog. The Gestapo would round up people in
the streets: one had to be careful. What if I didn't return
home? Zosia and Adam on their own!

I pass through a crowd standing in rows on both sides
of the burnt-out street, calling out what they have to
sell from the salvaged remains, from burnt-out shops:
'Pullovers, pullovers! Stockings! Stockings!' They are all
lightly dressed and can't stand still in this terrible cold.
Stomping, they call out in doom-laden voices with a
tragic emphasis on every word. I slip past quickly,
gathering that strange vision of sweaters and silk
stockings which, ironically, have survived to cause
these wretched survivors to perform a terrible *danse
macabre* in the light of the January sun, which exposes
the whole tragedy of this misery.

The fairy tale about the child which went into a forest
on a frosty day in search of diamonds in the sparkling
snow.

The sun is setting and a weeping woman cries:
'They've taken my son to a labour camp and I don't
even know where!' A tall man stands against the wall of
the Warsaw Philharmonic and accompanies himself
beautifully on an accordion. Further on, a band is
playing a waltz with such verve that you feel like
dancing in order to forget the terrible reality. The

streets are playing and singing to earn bread but are not dancing. Dearest Warsaw! The Royal Castle in ruins, its beautiful Assembly Hall gone: after the last ball there I lingered on in order to fix its beauty in my memory for ever.

I have no strength left, my legs ache, I rush home, where it's cold, the walls are covered in hoar frost and breath turns into steam. We get the evening meal ready and go to bed in order not to have to think, in order to forget it all. But like a nightmare, that *danse macabre* has got hold of my tortured imagination and weaves itself around me. I fall asleep but wake up often and hear 'Pullovers for sale! Pullovers for sale!'

In the courtyard a German soldier sits guarding the warehouse with its wooden ramp which is ideal for playing on. He calls me over, draws me onto his knee and gives me a sandwich. I am suddenly horrified at my compliance and, full of shame, I struggle free.

In the summer of 1940 the Gestapo order us out of the house which is coveted by a favourite of theirs. We move into aunt Janka Świtalska's villa in Mokotów opposite a deep grassy ditch and a mound which hides a military airfield. There, with one short interval in June 1941, we shall remain during the rest of our time in occupied Warsaw. The spacious villa, in a row of similar villas, is Bauhaus-modern, on two floors with a verandah and a basement. There is a large garden with a high wire fence and a remote-controlled gate. Myszka has been annoying mother, so she is given the sack and she now disappears from my life.

Aunt Janka is mother's elder sister. Like her, she married one of Piłsudski's loyal soldiers, who as well as a distinguished military career, held a number of important political appointments, including those of Mayor of Kraków, Speaker of the Sejm and Prime Minister. Aunt Janka is a great anglophile: she reads Galsworthy's novels and visited England before the war, once as head of the Polish girl guide contingent at an international jamboree. In the twenties she worked in the Polish legation in Helsinki and later was secretary to the wife of Józef Mościcki, the last pre-war head of state.

Aunt Janka's son Jacek – he who in those dream-like pre-war days had incited me to lock myself up in the bathroom – is now a teenager whom I worship. Occasionally he bullies me, occasionally we play at air raids. By their drones, as well as their shapes, we can quickly identify a Dornier transport, a Maesserschmidt fighter or a Junkers bomber. One day we get excited at seeing a Polish military bi-plane flying low, pursued by a German fighter, but we soon realise it is only a German exercise out of the Mokotów airfield.

The area is under Luftwaffe control. Unlike the Gestapo, the airforce has a reputation of being almost human, and when they come to search the villa for males hiding from the authorities and line us up against the walls of the hall, they are courteous and apologetic, and Zosia bursts into a giggle when one of them pompously opens the door to the downstairs toilet and looks embarrassed. There is a moment of tension when mother trips and stumbles down the stairs. But the farce conceals a potentially serious and dangerous situation. Because this is a daytime search and the villa stands in its own grounds, Jacek was able to spot them surrounding the house in good time. This gave aunt Janka time to burn incriminating documents. Mysterious bulletins have been appearing in the house from

Left: Uncle Świtalski during his
premiership, with Marshal Piłsudski
c. 1929

Above: Grandmother Paulina and
grandfather Adolf Tynicki with aunt
Janka and mother

Previous page: Myself in Warsaw
c. 1938

Above: Grandfather Adolf

Grandmother Karolina Czerniawska

Above: My parents' wedding day, 27th
April 1921

Left: Mother's portrait by Jan Rudnicki

Overleaf: Aunt Janka in 1926

time to time and the villa has been used as a safe-house for Polish military personnel. Latterly aunt sheltered Colonel Kazimierz Glabisz of the Army General Staff, who later made his escape to England, but currently there is no one in the basement. They are also looking for Jews and, as Zosia recalls, one of them offers us the thought that he hopes there aren't any 'Since the Jews don't take such risks for Poles'. Because aunt has these ties with the Resistance, she can always satisfy cook Henia's insatiable thirst for news about 'Mr Hoorhill's' latest initiatives.

On 5th September uncle Kazio, aunt Janka's husband, borrowed his colleague Colonel Lipiński's uniform and left Warsaw to fight on the Eastern Front as a volunteer, ending up at the Brześć Fortress which surrendered to General Guderian's panzers on 17 September. The fortress lay on the Soviet-German partition line. When the Germans and the Russians divided their spoils, uncle was made a German prisoner-of-war on account of his driving skills: the Germans needed drivers to help them transport prisoners back to the Reich. He thus escaped the Katyń Wood executions of Polish officers perpetrated by the Russians. He will spend the rest of the war a prisoner and when released by the Allies will choose to return to Poland, where the Communists will torture him and keep him in prison from 1948 till 1956. Released from prison he will die in a road accident in Warsaw in December 1962.

Uncle Konstanty, aunt Janka's younger brother, also lives at the villa. In a tiny dark-room upstairs he develops the photographs he takes with his precious Leica. It is a room full of magic, especially when a dim red bulb glows in the darkness and images begin to form on the white sheets of paper which swim in little trays on the work bench. He also has a thick crayon, blue at one end, red at the other, with which he underscores important passages in books and newspapers. He wears pince-nez glasses, is tall and thin, looking even thinner in his irreplaceable black suit, and always walks very fast. There is a large photograph of him in this suit in the blazing heat of the Egyptian desert with the Pyramids in the background. He is an intrepid traveller, a collector of maps and guides, had visited Westminster Abbey and the Isle of Wight, as well as the Holy Land. In the twenties he would volunteer himself as ballast on trial flights of lightweight planes operating between Warsaw and Lwów. Perhaps it is our perception of him as a vulnerable eccentric that prompts us to steal rolls of his discarded film, which we then throw back into his room in the form of the most disgusting stink-bombs. After the war he would send me huge parcels of books to enhance my library of Polish classics and reference books.

There is now a severe shortage of meat in the capital. A farmer is caught trying to smuggle in a pig dressed up as his wife. One evening a lorry reverses into our sloping drive and a herd of pigs is released to stampede into the basement garage. Jacek, Zosia and I spend hours trying to push one reluctant pig upstairs to surprise the adults in the dining room, but they fail to appreciate the joke as they chase it grunting across the slippery parquet floor. The pig too has little time to be amused for soon the house is filled with a sweet stench of slaughter and carcasses festoon all available basement space.

Father's mother, grandmother Karolina Czerniawska (born Salawa) from Tarnów, announces a visit. She is a formidable lady, mother of three, widowed early when grandfather, a railway worker, contracted gangrene after a train accident at the age 'at which Christ had died'. One of her grandchildren, Zbyszek is among the first Auschwitz victims as inmate No.72; one of her two sons-in-law, a policeman, had disappeared without trace during the German *blitzkrieg*. With her widowed daughter Lilka she runs a left-luggage depository on Tarnów railway station.

We three think it would be great fun to stuff grandmother's bed with upturned scrubbing brushes, so that she jumps up screaming when she lies down. In the event, her great bulk crushes all obstacles and she falls asleep unperturbed. The real excitement occurs a little earlier. It is past police curfew and we have given up waiting for her, when she suddenly appears, driven in a cab, late at night, totally oblivious of the occupying power's edicts. From her voluminous bags she unloads piles of home-made goodies and toys.

In running away from Kraków with Piłsudski's Legions, father was also running away from the stifling disciplinarian Catholicism of southern Poland and from his indomitable mother, whose family included Aniela Salawa, now on course for beatification by the Church. At the end of the First World War he was back in Warsaw, making rapid progress in the civil and ministerial service after a spell as Prime Minister Wojciechowski's personal treasurer and as administrative officer in Marshal Piłsudski's Belvedere Palace. In 1939 he was preparing to leave public life for a career in business.

After his successful escape to Romania, father makes his way to Turkey via Italy. He is clearly a skilled escapologist: during the Great War he had escaped from an Austrian internment camp in Hungary. He now sends us parcels with Turkish Delight and Halva packed in exotically decorated pale-blue-and-silver metal boxes. Then father sends money and mother is summoned by the Gestapo for breaking currency regulations. She manages to talk herself out of a journey to a concentration camp by demonstrating that she had not actually collected the money from an intermediary in Warsaw. On occasions like that her strategy, no doubt inspired by terror, is to talk rapidly and confusedly in order to demonstrate to the bewildered interrogating official that it is in his own self-interest to let her go if he wants to retain his mental equilibrium. She returns home shattered, worried by father's failure to understand the German new order in Poland. Father was born a citizen of the Austro-Hungarian Empire, which although one of Poland's nineteenth-century occupying powers, exercised a rule that was fair and benign in comparison with that of the Russians and the Prussians. By temperament and upbringing he was himself quite an authoritarian and as chairman of a government weights and measures standards committee in the thirties found the Berlin model of efficiency particularly attractive. He could never quite grasp the possibility that Hitler might have destroyed the German social order. But then he was not alone in being slow to realise that Germans were capable of organising crematoria as well as weights and measures.

His innocence had an important positive consequence. Brimming with his customary optimism, he sets about trying to get us out of Poland. He trusts that this can be achieved completely legally, although with the aid of some string-pulling and bribes. He uses friends in diplomatic missions and his pre-war Balkan tobacco trade contacts, he petitions Cardinal Hlond, the Primate of Poland who was his moral tutor at school, he pleads with the Italian legate at the Vatican, he has an audience with the Papal Nuncio in Turkey, Archbishop

Roncalli, the future Pope John XXIII, who has a good relationship with Franz von Papen, the Catholic German ambassador in Ankara. Mother is doing her bit taking on the Gestapo-controlled bureaucracy in Warsaw. She usually goes out for the whole day and we wait anxiously for her return. Sometimes she arrives with a box of delicious pastries from Lardelli's famous patisserie, which operates as though the war had never happened. Zosia too is hopeful and drills Rozetka in proper behaviour on long train journeys by teaching her how to use the toilet. One day, when the bathroom door is shut, she does a puddle outside the door.

Random memories

I float paper boats in the garden pool. Watching their progress intently, I lose my balance and fall in.

I establish a hostile contact with a boy in the street; his mother intervenes and, as I run to the safety of our fenced garden, she yells, 'I'll pull the legs off your arse!'

As the autumnal winds blow harshly across the open fields I am puzzled to know whence they come, given there are no trees here to set the air in motion.

The winds bring snows; crowds gather with sledges to slide into the Fort ditch. Against maternal advice, I grab a sledge and take an exhilarating ride.

Our neighbours have an affectionate St Bernard dog who greets me by putting his paws on my shoulders and I collapse under the weight.

Aunt Janka's blue willow-pattern dinner service depicts Chinamen laboriously crossing an awkwardly structured bridge. As there is no tea, she pours essence of apple peel into the china cups.

CHAPTER 5

A chronicle of non-events

*Formalities on the way to freedom: mother in
Warsaw reports to father successively in Bucharest,
Rome, Sofia and Istanbul*

1940

15 January: I have no desire to leave.
26 January: I am in a terrible uncertainty regarding the
journey because so long as there is cash it's quite all
right here, I have my friends and acquaintances. It
would be lovely to be with you but to subsist on little
money abroad, I'm not sure it's sensible to travel so far.
Again on the road on my own with the children,
sleepless nights. . .
27 January: I am in a terrible uncertainty as to what to
do with myself, should I undertake such a long journey,
will I arrive safely? Won't I be in a worse situation than
before? Are you in a position to earn enough to keep us
all? I could start on the formalities.
30 January: I'm still uncertain as to what to do with
myself. I've already gathered some information regarding the travel; it's important to have the consent of the
Foreign Ministry in Rome: this would be the basis for
my getting permission here, and of course there are still
many other formalities, certification that I am penniless,

confirmation that I am not in arrears with my taxes.

5 February: I can't somehow see my journey, there are so many formalities to be settled, I'm not sure I could cope.

9 February: Having thought it over at length, I've decided to come. I have the passports, so I am starting on the formalities, there is no other solution, although I could start a shop and then I could maintain myself and the children. I fear you won't be able to cope with us: please tell me frankly whether you've now got used to not having a family.

14 February: Yesterday was five [six] months since we parted and I don't know when I shall reach you, whether we'll be allowed out. Mrs Bielobradek has already gone, so maybe I'll also be lucky, though it will be hard to leave the flat with its memories; unfortunately my soul is Romantic and at every step it renews its memories, bad and joyful, from our last pleasant years. One must become a realist and not get sentimental over every trifle, for life is short, and it's a pity to lose the moments when we and the children could be together. For my exit I need to have a certificate of my non-Jewish origins and the consent of the Italian Interior Ministry. So you must deal with these matters in Rome, most importantly you must have enough to keep us and be able to show that we won't be a burden on the state. Janka is having a very difficult time, she wants to send Jacek abroad – perhaps they could both travel with us? Here they don't know the price of a ticket to Rome.

25 February: I can't get the money out of the bank, so I shall start selling the furniture. Maybe I'll sell it all, so that I have money for the journey – what do you think? What am I to do with your clothes, shall I bring them?

29 February: Could Janka and Jacek come with us?

3 March: I'm terribly pleased I've decided on this

important step. Yesterday I went to the lawyer who is sorting out the formalities connected with our travel. I keep urging Janka to go – is that possible?

5 March: I'm working on the travel arrangements, but my heart pounds with trepidation when I think of the journey, whether it makes sense to wander through the world with the children.

6 March: I might be able to make use of the Italian Consulate in Warsaw. I have hardly any cash left, I am still uncertain what to do, though inclined to come. I think we'll leave in April. Francopol is organising the whole trip for 1,000 złoty.

14 March: I went to Francopol today. They issue tickets only as far as Treviso [on the Austrian-Italian border]. I haven't got the visa yet. I imagine the formalities will take another month.

19 March: I chase around getting ready for the journey, though I still haven't got the visa and I check almost daily. I've organised Zosia's x-ray, and tomorrow I shall go to the office to collect a certificate that Zosia needs to be operated on by Dr Putti in Bologna. I've already got the extract from the Population Census and on Wednesday I'll receive the certificate that I am not in arrears with my taxes: how fortunate, I always made sure to be up-to-date! Also, on Wednesday I'll see the lawyer to complete an application for a passport. Janka would like to stay here till September, but an application for her travel could be put in motion.

26 March: Still no visa, I have a premonition I won't be travelling.

31 March: Still no sign of the visa – probably our plans will come to nothing. Where am I to go? Perhaps I should buy three pills and cut short this wretched existence.

13 April: Today I'll get news about the visa.

20 April: I was thrilled that you are making such strenuous efforts on my behalf, but here things are at a standstill.

21 April: I've seen a couple of lawyers. Still no visa and not having it blocks further preparations.

13 May: I've got the visa now and am applying for permission to leave.

20 May: I have the Romanian visa – the papers are deposited in the Office – the application [for permission to leave?] may take from between two weeks to two months. I have no money to pay the travel agency so I must sell something urgently.

26 May: I get the impression there is now doubt about my travel because apparently they don't issue [exit] permits.

29 May: Perhaps I'll get a job as a waitress, I'm making every effort to remain in Warsaw. As for coming to you, we'll have to wait a while. That's what they are advising in the Office.

3 June: My departure is still in doubt.

6 June: Since refugees are allowed to return, maybe you too could return to the old den?

17 June: I'm doing everything to be able to come, especially now since I shall soon lose the flat. I do believe I'll come and we shall meet soon.

19 July: I still don't know when I shall get the permit.

22 July: [Exit] permits are not issued. Adam Nebelski lent me 200 złoty but this is a pittance, the children are always hungry, they want meat and fruit and it's heartbreaking when I have no money for the purchases.

31 July: A fortune-teller told me my travel is problematic.

16 August: I don't know how much you earn, whether we are to live in one room, and are you in a position to maintain us?

9 September: The German authorities have issued the exit permit, so I can go. Send me the Turkish visa and find out what else needs doing and what our route will be. We are coming in three weeks!

5 October: We need an official declaration regarding the Turkish visa for the German authorities; I still don't know when I shall be ready to go, since the travel agency is still negotiating various formalities. The declaration regarding the Turkish visa has to be sent on, just as in the case of the Romanian visa.

12 October: I don't know whether I'll be able to afford to buy tickets all the way to Istanbul. The travel agency told me that they'll sort out the exit formalities in a couple of days. We need to have guarantees of visas and official declarations for the countries through which I am to travel, and for the country of my destination. I've decided on a mad step, on a journey, and I observe our wretched children, how will I cope with them, how will they stand the journey?

31 October: I am still waiting for the passport and I don't know why it's taking so long. I've done everything in my power and now I am waiting patiently.

8 December: I've telegraphed Vienna regarding the visa guarantees, I am now waiting and then I'll be able to go.

24 December: At the Paßstelle they again gave a different story: it's to be transferred to the following address: Amt des General-Gouvernement, Abt. Paßstelle, Krakau. To be paid only into the Reichsbank and only in Turkish currency.

31 December: Should I give up the plan? Is there a sense in tramping around with the children?

1941

7 January: The Paßstelle Office requires proof of payment. I've cabled that you should send the receipt to the Paßstelle in Kraków. I've been informed that my case has been referred with the visas to Kraków for a decision. I worry because the visas will expire and all my efforts will come to nothing. Maybe we are not fated to be reunited.

13 January: I was told at the Paßstelle they'll let me know when the papers are returned after a decision. In Kraków the lawyer and [sisters-in-law] Herta and Anita are pressing for a definite yes or no. I don't believe I'll get the exit permit. Uncertainty is the worst. I am pursuing all the formalities myself as I can't afford the travel office. Pity, because Meer is quick and efficient. My God, what shall we do if we are not allowed to go!

23 January: I must now wait on the decision from Kraków. What am I to do when the Bulgarian visa expires?

28 January: I still have no decision about my departure and I am just waiting.

30 January: I still have no reply regarding my departure.

3 February: I went to the Paßstelle, where they told me that I am certain to go, but must wait, so I am waiting patiently.

7 February: At the Paßstelle they keep telling me I am certain to leave. The lawyer came with me and advised me to petition Kraków again and this I've done.

15 February: Don't worry about us and don't send telegrams, because as you know, I hate them! With the help of Janka and other good people I am managing better and better, so be reassured. So I beg you don't waste money on telegrams, calm down because your worry and your concern may lead me to a nervous breakdown. There is no point in urging us to move without a passport and an exit permit – if I had them I certainly wouldn't be delaying my departure. Please forgive me for writing harshly but I see it's better to be guided by common sense.

1 March: I am waiting for the exit permit.

7 March: My Dear, but what can I do if I still haven't got the passport? Pani Rodys is also preparing to go, she is very confident she'll go.

18 March: They told me at the Paßstelle yesterday that I could travel via Russia, but I think I'll give up. I would need a transit visa, but I don't have any money or appetite for further efforts.

22 March: I've just received your telegram in which you propose a different route, but I can't go that way, only, as the Paßstelle officials told me, through Russia.

31 March: Don't be upset that nothing's come of our journey.

25 April: I keep pressing for the passport and I still have hope that, despite everything, we'll be able to go. Sunday is our jubilee, twenty years of marriage. I'll drink a bottle of wine which I got from Herta and Anita.

27 April: Pani Rodys maintains we'll certainly go. She is making a great effort and says she won't abandon me and we'll leave together. God! She has so much faith!

10 May: I am still waiting for a reply from Vienna regarding the guarantees for the Romanian and Hungarian visas.

17 May: I now have the passport and I can go. But the passport needs to be returned to Kraków for a couple of days, because they forgot to stamp it, but I've seen it and it was a nice feeling. I can buy tickets only as far as the Hungarian border, so you'll have to organise the journey beyond. At Meer they advise taking a car from Budapest to Bucharest, but everywhere one needs money. My passport is valid until 7 November. Tell Herta and Anita to await me in Vienna. The children are so happy that they'll see you! The dog's coming too.

28 May: I don't know when exactly I'll be able to go, because the passport is still in Kraków, where it was sent for stamping. Don't buy the tickets until I tell you I actually have the passport.

3 June: I still have no passport.

11 June: I am packed and I am only waiting for the passport extension and I think we may be on our way in ten days.

17 June: I am hoping for the passport any day now.

24 June: Another piece of bad luck regarding our travel. I went to the Paßstelle for the passport, I'm supposed to get some sort of answer on Thursday.

1st July: Regarding my travel there is silence, it's bound to come about one day, but for the time being one has to wait. I've stopped pestering them. The passport is valid till 15th July.

FATHER ADDS: In December 1940 my wife cabled that she would be granted a passport with a right to leave Poland on payment of US $1,800 into the Reichsbank in Berlin. Thanks to the help of friends whom I was lucky enough to have abroad, I collected the sum and in January I transmitted this sum from Istanbul to Berlin. I will not dwell on the various complications my wife had to face during the following six-months' period, during which her passport was being issued, until 1 June when she was summoned to collect it, only to be told that it expired that very day and that she would have to wait for its renewal. And when she eventually had it renewed, on 22 June Hitler attacked Russia and the Istanbul tourist office recalled the railway tickets it had sent to Vienna, which caused untold difficulties when she eventually set out for Turkey. The difficulties were considerable because only German citizens could purchase such tickets, and in any event they could not be bought with the 10 złoty my wife was allowed for the journey.

CHAPTER 6

The author in the eyes of two of the women in his life

*Mother and Zosia reporting to father
during December 1939–June 1941*

ZOSIA: Adam said you will probably be surprised that mummy was clever enough to get us through.

MOTHER: Serious and pensive, Adam endures the discomforts of this life; he reads a lot and counts and I have great satisfaction from his cleverness.

ZOSIA: Adam is spoilt: when mother scolds him, he laughs. Panna W brings him up one way and mother another way. So in the end Adam doesn't know whether he is in the right or in the wrong. At this moment he is playing [the piano] under mother's supervision. My surgeon is in Romania, my leg is all right. Adam is insufferable.

MOTHER: Adam is very intrigued by a doll that can close its eyes. The children are still reliving our adventures, while I sometimes have the feeling it was a terrible dream.

MOTHER: Adaś fluently read through the card [which I

have just written to you] and says: 'Why did you put the year on? Surely daddy knows it is 1940.'

ZOSIA: I tell you truly, it would be easier to write a letter during an earthquake than in our bedlam, because Adam is jumping up and down on the table, mummy is playing [the piano] to destruction, Panna Władysława is whistling like a nightingale, it's quite unbearable.

MOTHER: Adaś often sings to himself. He's learnt naughty poems, as these things will cling to children. He is a monkey but he has a nice voice, perhaps he will be famous.

ZOSIA: Adam goes into the courtyard on his own and has learnt a beautiful poem which he recited during supper. Here it is:

> Oh my heart, oh my spouse,
> When I die all's yours,
> Everything in the house
> And the trousers on my —

It's poems like these he has no trouble remembering.

ZOSIA: I've already done part of my homework so I can write to you a bit. Mummy is gone to see the Bergiel people. Adam went there once and saw their cats which wander everywhere, so he said these cats walk everywhere like flies.

ZOSIA: Write me lots of letters with interesting stamps, but don't send interesting ones on postcards because it's a pity to tear them off. Adam keeps teasing Rozetka.

I must warn you, Daddy, if you wish to have me, Rozetka must come too.

ZOSIA: Today, instead of Adam, it is Rozetka that's performing acrobatically: walking along parapets, over my desk and across this card. Adam is a nuisance and it's difficult writing this letter. Would you like me to bring the canary and the fish in the bowl as well?

ZOSIA: As I am writing this letter to you, the house is unusually quiet because (thank God!) Jacek and Adam are asleep, although it seems Adam still isn't because he is mumbling to himself. If you can, send as many parcels as possible and send me one too.

MOTHER: It's good that you are going to the country of famous singers [Italy], perhaps you too will at last begin to sing and astonish people with your baritone voice. Adam too hums often – maybe when we go on our vagabondage again we'll become itinerant showpeople – what do you think?

MOTHER: At this moment great rejoicing: three parcels have arrived. Adaś dictates: 'Thank you Daddy for the parcel and I kiss you.' We'll have a spaghetti feast.

MOTHER: Adam is very independent and like you he can't do without soda water. Sometimes I buy him a little syphon and he immediately struggles with it to his room. He's now very thin.

MOTHER: It's hard for the children to be without a father, but Adaś looks well, and as for looking thin – he's taken after me.

MOTHER: I've collected the figs. Adaś kissed me on account of the parcel. He is a very interesting child. He reads already, counts, plays cards and is very polite. Jacek is not bored in his company despite the great difference in age. Zosia grumbles a lot.

MOTHER: I long for the children to be with you because you have so much patience. Adam needs male guidance because he is becoming unruly, but he is decent and is excellent at playing patience though he is only five. He is very clever. Pity you can't be here to admire him.

MOTHER: The children are healthy and pleasant and often tease their mummy because they have a sense of humour.

MOTHER: Adaś thanks you for the sweets in a beautiful box.

ZOSIA: Adam now manages to say 'r' instead of 'w', but now for a change he stutters, but only when he speaks very fast. As for writing, he can just about manage it. Once he even wrote a card to his nanny.

MOTHER: Adam is small and a dark horse, he misses you in a different way, but he certainly remembers you, although he's got attached to Kocio who brings him whatever he can. He bought Adaś a pair of shoes, brings him sweets almost daily and this attracts a child. I'll send you the photographs Kocio has taken. The children have grown up a lot. Zosia reaches up to my eyebrows, while Adaś reaches halfway up my arm. Zosia is a brave and lovable girl, she is strict with Adaś and helps me a lot with bringing him up.

MOTHER: Since yesterday we are staying with the Felixes because Adaś is reacting badly to the Soviet bombing nearby.

It is now summer 1941 and columns of German infantry and armour rumble through Warsaw's main streets day and night on the way east. People who in desperation try to cross their path after waiting for hours get beaten up or shot. Hitler attacks the Soviet Union. The Russians begin sporadic bombings and we shelter with friends away from the airfield. I get very frightened and nervous and mother gives me Valerian drops every night to calm me down. After a spate of these wanderings through Warsaw, mother decides we might as well go back to aunt Janka's villa, especially now that the threat of wholesale bombardments seems to have passed.

But with the opening of the eastern front our last chance to leave appears to have gone. Then suddenly, after eighteen months of endless encounters with bureaucracies, permission to travel is granted for the three of us and the dog and on 8 July 1941 we board a train for Vienna. Aunt Janka, ever alert to international strategic and political developments, wants mother to report to her when Japan joins the war. The coded message mother is to write is: 'I have stained my new leather gloves'. I don't suppose that in view of Pearl Harbour mother felt the need to make use of the code, assuming she ever remembered it given the overwhelming pressure of more immediate problems that beset her.

PART TWO

Warsaw to Istanbul

(July 1941–January 1942)

Train travel is exhilarating and, as we cross the border of the General-Gouvernement, the rump of what barely two years ago was free Poland, into the German Reich proper on the way to Vienna, I am not at all conscious of the possibility that I may be leaving my native land for ever, and consequently I feel no pain. But I shall never see Jacek again: he will die on 1 August 1944, on the first day of the Warsaw Uprising, burnt by a flamethrower while attacking a German tank. His last words to a fellow-soldier, who was urging him to run away, were: 'Here they ordered me to stand, here I shall stay.' A little earlier he had escaped from a prison hospital where he had been operated on after being shot by a German soldier while escaping from an interrogation. He was not expected to walk again but the Polish surgeons in the hospital performed the impossible. My cousin Jola, aunt Herta's daughter, will die for lack of medical care. My cousin Zbyszek will die at Auschwitz, one of its earliest and youngest victims. In one of his letters to his mother from the camp he wonders whether his aunt Marysia [my mother] had

reached Turkey and hopes to be home soon. Uncle
Kazio will for ever remain a symbol and a historical
figure rather than a human being, though his letters to
me after release from prison in 1956 will offer a brief
glimpse from behind the mask of history.

In Vienna mother discovers that, because of the
German invasion of the Soviet Union, our tickets for
further rail travel have been withdrawn from the
Viennese travel agency. It isn't clear whether it was the
agency or father, or both, who thought that war in the
east would compel us to abandon our journey at the
last minute. So now we are stranded, or even worse
than stranded: we have nowhere to go. On leaving
mother had to sign an undertaking that we would
never return; there was a strict time limit on our right to
stay in Austria; and now we have lost our ability to
travel further. So we go to St Stephen's Cathedral to
pray for a miracle. The miracle is performed by aunt
Herta, who, being Czech, is a citizen of the German
Reich and is therefore allowed to purchase railway
tickets on our behalf. We celebrate by taking a ride on
the Riesenrad, the famous big wheel in the Viennese
amusement park. Mother now spots my talent for
orienteering in large cities, so whenever she can, she
takes me on visits to consulates and travel bureaux.

From Vienna we travel to Budapest, where we are
met by father's friend Pan Myśliński, a genial Pole
representing the Polish-Hungarian Friendship Society,
who had promised father to look after us in the
Hungarian capital, where there is still a sizeable group
of Polish refugees who escaped in 1939.

Mother, constantly under severe stress, takes me
everywhere now that I have demonstrated my orienteering skills. I am happy to explore new and exciting
cities with her, particularly the imposing Hungarian

capital with its trams that cross the wide Danube and its neat underground trains. We jump into one, just as it is about to go, leaving Pan Myśliński stranded on the platform. Mother hasn't noticed and doesn't believe me when I tell her: when an inspector arrives she confidently tells him the gentleman at the far end of the carriage has our tickets. But I am right and mother is eventually shocked to discover that we are not only guilty of fare-dodging but are also lost in a strange city. This little adventure has a happy ending: Pan Myśliński soon catches up with us at the next station.

Another individual who catches up with us is a member of the Polish Secret Service who wants mother to act as courier for secret messages to Polish agents in Istanbul. Flights between Budapest and Istanbul regularly used by the Service have just been suspended. One message, a report from the Home Army in Warsaw, comes concealed in a large Odol toothpaste tube, wrapped in paper with the instruction: 'To be delivered to the lady who sings in Istanbul, Ayaz Pasha 26'. (Father later chafes at these risky, simple-minded cloak-and-dagger methods.) The other consists of a handwritten report from the local representative of the Polish Government in Exile in London. Mother is very uneasy at having to perform this mission but her anxieties are lessened when Zosia offers to rewrite the second report in her minuscule handwriting on wafer-thin sheets which she coils round an empty spool and then covers with thread. The spool then travels first in a workbasket, then concealed in the train toilet. Pan Myśliński has put us on the train for Bucharest. I shall see him again briefly a decade or so later in London when he unexpectedly calls on us. I shall stare at him in wonder and amazement, not knowing what to say, except to thank him for the nice toy (what was it? a large green tractor?) that he gave me in Budapest.

We arrive in Bucharest by train in the evening and book into a comfortable hotel but there is a Soviet air raid in the middle of the night and we rush into the basement for shelter. During the day we go on visits to a magnificent baroque villa on a leafy boulevard as guests of Józef Beck, the Polish Foreign Minister, and his wife, who have been interned by the Romanians after escaping from Poland, and there are soldiers on guard outside. He is a gaunt, remote figure, gravely ill and shattered by Poland's collapse. She is lively and energetic, and because the house-arrest does not apply to her, she is free to help mother in the next stage of her battles with officialdom. So my services as city-guide are dispensed with and I am given a pile of fashion magazines to pass the time, but the two huge gilded mirrors in the hall, which multiply my image into infinity, are a far greater attraction. Meanwhile Zosia characteristically observes the local low life. She notes that in Bucharest restaurants waiters are summoned like dogs with a clucking sound and that they respond by shouting words which to her sensitive ears sound like familiar Polish obscenities.

Mother now spends days in tackling the Bulgarians who steadfastly refuse to grant us visas. Mr Zlotarev, father's pre-war Bulgarian business acquaintance, had promised to look after us in Sofia. But mother has now given up hope of ever meeting him, and as she is about to leave the Bulgarian consulate for the last time, she asks whether as a favour they could send Mr Zlotarev a telegram telling him not to expect us. Noting mother's distress, the official agrees and asks for details. When he hears the name of the addressee he becomes agitated, doesn't even want to note down his address and asks mother to return the next day. When she does, she is informed that visas have been granted. Hardly believing her luck, mother prefers not to spoil it by asking for an explanation of this reversal but takes advantage of the new attitude of servility to request the official to cable Mr Zlotarev to be sure he is there at Sofia station to meet us.

We are now free to leave: we shall not see minister Beck again, as he will die in humiliating captivity, but his widow will attend my wedding in London sixteen years later and will entertain the guests with accounts of how she used to bath and dress the bridegroom.

On the way to Bulgaria we leave the train to embark onto a ferry to cross the Danube and catch another train on the other side for Sofia. We arrive in the evening and pile out, eagerly scanning the blacked-out platform for signs of Mr Zlotarev, especially since mother was sold inadequate tickets in Bucharest and the railway inspector has impounded our passports because she had no more money left to pay the surcharge. The platform soon empties, leaving us with our bundles and the dog. At the far end stands a tall distinguished gentleman in a black suit, who at first observes us quizzically from a distance, and eventually approaches, asking in French: 'Are you Mme Czerniawska? My name is Zlotarev. I have no idea who you are, but I received instructions to meet you.' He pays the inspector and retrieves our passports.

We spend the night on one large soft bed in a luxury hotel. In the morning, surprised at his non-reappearance and worried about the hotel bill, mother goes to seek out Mr Zlotarev at his home address and is surprised to see how he has changed overnight. He too is startled to see her and tells her that the Bulgarian Deputy Foreign Minister is also called Zlotarev. She rushes off to the Ministry with a bunch of red roses for his wife which she bought with money she got from selling a piece of jewellery. There is amusement all round at mother's insistence, in the telegram sent from Bucharest, that the minister should come to meet her personally at the station. Years later the minister will himself become a refugee and will meet mother again in the American mid-west and reminisce over how a coincidence of names saved our expedition.

Somewhere beyond Sofia near the Turkish border the railway tracks peter out. We climb into a cart: on the way huge shadowy outlines of Greek mountains appear on our right. At the frontier there is haggling and squabbling with the owner of a large black limousine (like the one in which we escaped from Warsaw) over fares to Istanbul and the allocation of the few available seats. Eventually, we all squeeze in with three or four other people, a polyglot group, which includes a voluble incarnation of Mata Hari and an American.

The road runs through hilly country. The driver appears to have problems with his steering wheel; he keeps lifting and snapping it into place with a sharp bang before each bend, and sometimes right in the middle of a bend. In a Turkish village we have our first meal in freedom. In a roomy, airy hall some twenty guests sit round a colossal dish from which we all sup with devilishly long spoons. The village is dilapidated and dirty, and as we pass through others like it, I begin to wonder whether this month-long journey into the unknown was worth it. As the evening approaches, excitement mounts and suddenly someone calls out a strange word several times over. Years later, reading Xenophon's account in *Anabasis* of Greek soldiers, escaped from Persian captivity, going wild at reaching the familiar Black Sea at last and crying 'Thalassa,

thalassa!', I realise this is the word the man called out as we approached Istanbul.

I grow apprehensive at the thought of meeting the man who is my father, a dimly remembered figure in his formal three-piece suit, whom I had not seen for almost two years. But as we arrive at his lodgings, he is not there: he had no idea when, if ever, we would arrive, so, not expecting us, he had gone out on some errand. When he does arrive, I huddle in a corner stunned and perplexed.

It's too expensive for us to stay in Istanbul, so we move across the Sea of Marmara to the Asiatic side. We first occupy a room in a cottage. Zosia soon befriends a hedgehog which runs around the room at night whistling and leaving behind pools of green liquid. Father attacks it with his slipper. Perhaps it's this threat of an incipient menagerie that decides father on a move to Pension Apergis in Kadiköy on the corner of a street facing the sea, which has a promenade overlooking cliffs rising from a sandy beach. From our windows at the top of the house we have panoramic views of the ancient walled city of Istanbul which dominates the skyline with minarets and domes and at sunset glows with light reflected from the surrounding waters. I make a daring descent down a steep footpath to the beach. I come across a broken piece of triangular glass. The sun-lit colourful world of the Mediterranean now appears even more exotic when perceived through this prism which gives all objects glowing multi-coloured outlines. I lost this glass a long time ago but I have never stopped looking for it.

I have a small collection of oddly assorted books, few of them with any good pictures to look at. The films at the local cinema are not much better: one can barely discern the cowboys shooting it out but the impact is nevertheless powerful enough for me to emerge from the darkness to jump onto my scooter and shout 'Bang! Bang!'. The shining red-and-yellow machine, which runs smoothly on its elegant spoked wheels with ball-bearings, is my prize possession. It's a gift from one of father's many acquaintances, an expansive Greek, reputedly the master of a dozen languages, including some Polish. Another acquaintance is Pani Mochnacka, a middle-aged spinster who has a neat tiny flat furnished Turkish-style where she serves Turkish coffee while through her window I observe a muezzin intoning from the balcony of a small mosque close by.

On Sundays we take a paddle-steamer for outings to Istanbul. Occasionally we board the ancient dark-green overground train which pretends to be under-ground, Istanbul's only attempt at a metro system, which pulls up-hill from near the bridge where the steamers dock to the centre of town. We explore the maze of covered alleyways which make up the city's bazaar, we visit the Hagia Sofia mosque with its magnificent Koran inscriptions blazing from the walls, but ignorant of history, I have no idea this was once a great Christian basilica. In our favourite coffee house I am allowed to have chocolate trifle, so long as I summon enough courage to order it in French as 'La soupe anglaise'.

Once we sail up the gently winding Bosphorus with its ranks of villas and palaces to the Polish embassy, where the Polish flag still flutters as though nothing had happened. Not far away is Adampol, the town named by the Turks in honour of the poet Adam Mickiewicz, who died of cholera in Istanbul in 1855 while trying to raise a Polish legion to liberate Poland from Russia already under threat from the British and the French in the Crimea.

This, however, is a country untouched by war and its agreeable climate helps to emphasise its distance from frozen, ruined Warsaw. But even idly sipping coffee in an open-air restaurant mother would suddenly say that we are being watched and followed. Father remains upset that she has not brought their wedding photograph. To no avail she keeps reminding him that as a one-time citizen of the benign Austro-Hungarian empire, he can't imagine the bestiality of Hitler's Germans, for whom the sight of a photograph of a Polish officer, signed by Marshal Piłsudski, in the possession of a person seeking to abandon the care and protection of the Third Reich, would provoke horrible consequences. Mother also develops her penchant for the occult: she persuades us to take part in séances and recalls ghost stories from her Ukrainian childhood. Consequently, I develop a fear of dark rooms which father hopes to dispel by reminding me that Marshal Piłsudski trained himself by force of will to enter them. Father also wants to try out on me a renowned ancient Polish remedy for chest infection: half a dozen wine glasses are held upside down over a burning candle to create a vacuum inside them and are then stuck in rows on the exposed back of the patient. They cling to the flesh and suck out the evil spirits. Somehow I manage to resist this awesome cure but I have my first taste of a fresh fig which I snatch from a branch overhanging a garden wall.

Father has a group of Polish friends, who have been watching his desperate and persistent efforts to get us out. The most interested is Pan Rodys, who had also been struggling to get his wife out of Poland. It was hoped she would travel with us, but he assumed the Germans' demand of a ransom was yet another blackmailing stalling tactic and, unlike father, could not face paying it. Some years have to pass before I begin to wonder whether it was right for father to bargain with the Germans. The eventual discovery that Jews had similarly bargained with them in order to save lives clears my conscience. I also have the nagging feeling that we should have remained with our countrymen in Poland and shared their fate. Meanwhile, Pan Rodys consoles himself with music: he composes a piano piece for mother called *Marmara*. The score, penned in his extravagant handwriting, is itself a work of art. Zosia too discovers an artistic talent: under the influence of constant family discussions as to what to do next, she sketches the family on various exotic journeys. The best one portrays us on camels in Bedouin clothes crossing the Sahara. Someone gives her a box of fragile and delicately tinted pastel crayons. They are housed in a small black cardboard box and the white-rimmed name sticker also portrays the subtle rainbow colours to be found inside. The crayons are not round like all normal crayons and pencils, but curiously oblong and wrapped in paper casings and are very brittle. However, it is clear that Zosia is best with vivid colours and sharp outlines, and the crayons are soon set aside, chipped and crumbling.

My first artistic attempts are also full of minarets and camels and vivid sunlight. The nights too are enchantingly bright: the stars are very numerous and very near, the full moon seems to hang just above the house. I ask how far it is. I also ask what the difference is between 'culture' and 'civilisation' and whether I had come out of mother's tummy. It is becoming clear to my parents that at six it is time I was sent to school. But which school? Father had used up all his savings to get us out of Poland and we are now running out of money. He even had to sell his portable typewriter: a sacrifice that impresses me. It looks as though after some six months in Turkey we shall be on the move again soon. But where? Such far-flung and disparate places as India, the United States and Palestine are considered.

Meanwhile, as winter approaches, the skies turn grey, the wind whistles in the panes of our exposed, unheated guest-house room, the seas are choppy and sometimes one of the many paddle-steamer ferries, which criss-cross the Marmara from Istanbul in various directions to harbours on Princes Islands and on the Asiatic side, is seen bobbing up and down with its giant wheels idle. One morning, the sea against the city walls is full of Italian Navy ships, which after a few days mysteriously disappear.

Although we know that America is the land of hope and opportunity where gold lies on pavements ready to be picked up, it appears a distant prospect on account of the quota system. As for India, father, who before the war had some association with the Czech shoe manufacturers Bata, had written to their Bengal branch, enquiring about employment prospects. At the end of January 1942 he receives a reply from the Managing Director, of which I quote the most encouraging part:

> The climate of the Province and the place in
> which the factory is situated is not considered to
> be very healthy and in fact one of the most
> unfavourable parts of India as far as climate is
> concerned. The temperature during the dry
> season reaches 106 degrees Fahrenheit and there
> are heavy monsoons during June, July and
> August during which time the atmosphere will be
> very heavy. Anyway the climate is not such that
> it could be borne by women and children. I may,

however, mention that many of them are leaving
to hill stations such as Darjeeling, Simla. etc.,
where most of the schools are situated. The
fooding and living expenses in such hill stations
are extremely high and only well-to-do people
can afford the same.'

But the letter comes when our bags are already packed
and we are awaiting a train from Istanbul which will
take us to Ankara and beyond on the way to Palestine.

PART THREE

The Middle East

(January 1942 – August 1947)

CHAPTER 7

Tel Aviv

(1942–1945)

We travel through Ankara in the middle of the night and the Turkish capital is ablaze with lights, some of them reflected in a wide river which we cross. I fall asleep and when I briefly wake up the moon is shining. But every few minutes the train plunges into a tunnel and when it emerges, there is a sheer drop along its side and jagged mountains loom above. During the day we travel through Syria and Lebanon, having lunch in a sumptuous restaurant car. I comment loudly that the man opposite looks like a frog. As luck would have it, he understands Polish, but is kindly enough not to take offence. Arriving in Palestine we lodge in a modestly furnished, whitewashed room in the centre of Tel Aviv.

The nucleus of a Polish Army has been formed in Syria. It moves to Palestine under British command, where it is swelled by people whom Stalin had agreed to release from the labour camps, where he had them deported when he decided to 'help' the Poles against Hitler in 1939. Now Stalin is himself in need of allied help in his desperate struggle against the invading German armies, and so he accedes to the Polish

Government-in-Exile's demand to have these people
released. During 1942-43 the wretched remnants of
those deportations make their way across the vast
expanses of the Soviet Union to end up in British
refugee camps in India and Persia. They swell the
colonies of Poles in Jerusalem and Tel Aviv and various
camps throughout Palestine. Many are young orphans
who look as emaciated as the victims of Belsen and
Auschwitz but, in the common struggle against the
Germans, the British authorities regard it as bad taste
to publicise the atrocities of the friendly and heroic
Soviet Union. Perhaps among those now recovering
under the Mediterranean sun are some of those whom
I heard calling out from sealed goods wagons in Soviet-
occupied Poland in the autumn of 1939.

So there is now a sizeable concentration of Poles in
Palestine and a network of Polish organisations springs
up: churches, schools, newspapers and a publishing
house devoted mainly to re-issuing Polish classics. Tel
Aviv and Jerusalem are full of Polish-speaking Jews
who had left Poland hoping for the creation of a Jewish
state. Not all of them are happy at seeing so many Polish
gentiles, who even keep their schools open on Satur-
days, and on Sundays sing hymns in a flat in the centre
of Tel Aviv, which they have converted into a chapel.
There are Polish soldiers milling around after mass and
Arab news-vendors sell the illustrated weekly *Parada*,
from which I learn that Poles are winning the war
single-handed. Much later, I learn that it is the British
who have won single-handed.

Somehow I had managed to absorb the image
propagated in the Nazi *Der Stürmer* newspaper of the
wizened, servile, sub-human Jew squatting in a wooden
shack, so the sight of bronzed, well-fed youths swarming
the bright modern avenues of Tel Aviv, and clearly

lording it over the Arabs, is very puzzling and instructive. Initially we lodge in the centre of the city, off Allenby Boulevard, within easy walking distance of the Polish school in Montefiore Street. There are about fifteen of us in a light airy classroom fronting the street, furnished with flat tables in a horseshoe pattern. Pani Fotygo is in charge: she is a slim, thin-faced woman, severe but kind. We learn to read and write, do sums and acquire the rudiments of English. When we have religious instruction, some pupils disappear for a session with a rabbi, while we have a black-cassocked priest. This is my first official encounter with the sinister representatives of the Catholic Church. Somehow he had learnt that I can be troublesome at home, so he tells me that he knows I don't love my mother. I am bewildered and deeply hurt but too young to free myself from the hold of this sadistic organisation: at Christmas I dutifully play a Polish shepherd (dressed in fur-lined jerkin) come to offer baby Jesus a dish of butter.

But my most vivid memory of that first school is of a drawing lesson. My landscape has several trees. Straight, brown trunks, rounded clumps of intensely green foliage and brilliantly orange oranges. Birds in the shapes of floppy black V-signs nestle in the foliage and circle in the air. The work appears finished. Suddenly, I take a thick black crayon to demarcate the brown trunks and the vivid foliage. Teacher is terribly upset and scolds me for ruining the picture with lines that don't exist on real trees.

After a brief period of squatting in the town centre, where, to my parents' great horror, I try out my scooter along the kerb of busy Allenby Boulevard, we move to Hajarkon 108. (We return to the hotel room briefly in January 1943 when our friendly landlords succeed in pushing us out temporarily.) This is an ornate two-storey

L-shaped villa on the corner of Hajarkon and Frishman. It has peeling caramel-coloured paint on its distinctive mouldings and balconies with bulging black-iron railings. It would look totally out of place amid modernist villas and blocks of white, pink and cream-coloured functional apartments had there not been another very similar old-fashioned villa across Frishman which, unlike ours, is surrounded by railings and an extensive formal garden. The neighbourhood is always teeming with people, especially raucous children including myself, but that mysterious garden, which is in full view of our balcony and which an unseen hand tends, stays still and empty. We have two rooms of a three-room flat on the first floor, with one small balcony, facing Frishman, and a larger 'kitchen' balcony overlooking the backyard. The kitchen balcony is of great strategic importance. I can use it to sneak out of the flat undetected if my parents are in the living room; also the tiny window of the lavatory overlooks the balcony, so you can lock yourself in the lavatory and then climb out of the window, leaving the rest of the family to resort to desperate measures. On the way out through the kitchen it is fun to fill to the brim with water all the glasses standing on the shelf: whoever hurriedly takes one down will get splashed.

The remaining room at the corner with a larger balcony skirting the two sides of the house belongs to our landlords, the Drymmers: he, a captain in the Polish Army, is a tall, gaunt, taciturn figure, always walking about in a dressing-gown (an intelligence officer, as I learn much later from his memoirs, with pre-war intelligence experience and strong anti-semitic inclinations). We first met him in this narrative as a Foreign Ministry official (in charge of the Ministry's evacuation from Warsaw); she, Pani Halina, an opulent blonde, her face shining from too much make-up, is my god-mother. Or rather, my second-best godmother, as I learn much later, for the first one, Maria Kosko, author of a study of the reception in France of Henryk Sienkiewicz's celebrated novel *Quo Vadis*, and of an exercise in anthropology, *Le fils assassiné*, turned out to be a Protestant and therefore unacceptable. On publication of my first book of poems she will send me a book of American verse as a present. Through the negligence of my publisher the book reaches me years later – after her death.

Halina Drymmer runs a beauty parlour; in her spare time she is a nurse in the Polish Army. After the war, she will have a triumphant career in cosmetics with Helena Rubinstein in Switzerland. The area beneath our shared flat houses a Tnuva milkbar with delicious keffirs variously flavoured. The remaining ground-floor area, facing Hajarkon, will soon house a family of Jewish refugees from a pogrom in Baghdad. I become very friendly with Joseph, the eldest of the four children, but they all puzzle me: they look and behave like Arabs and, suitably dressed, they would pass unnoticed in an Arab community.

Beyond our house, the stretch facing Hajarkon is a large dusty plot. At weekends it fills up with rows of assorted roaring military trucks, which disgorge bois-terous Australians, New Zealanders, Britons and, in due course, Americans. They make for the beaches, for the nightspots along Hajarkon and the NAAFI, which is just across the road, a long low building separated from the street by a wide border of lawns and flower beds. The giant Aussies get drunk pretty quickly and can be seen sleeping amid the flower beds, ready for the Military Police from a huge sinister maroon-coloured building further up Hajarkon. The MPs arrive in 15-cwt trucks, pick up the Aussies by their hands and feet and hurl them onto the metal floor on which they land with a loud thump. As for the flowers, our street gang has already picked them the night before and sold them to the soldiers when they were still sober and ready for adventure. In the late hours of the night I am kept awake by the heat, the roar of engines and the beams of headlights of trucks moving back to camps in the desert.

Hajarkon runs parallel with the sea shore, separated from the promenade by a row of buildings along the other side of Hajarkon and a sloping descent of sand dunes. The tarmacked lane to the promenade is a good racing track for my Turkish scooter, still the envy of my friends who have to make do with primitive wooden home-made contraptions on noisy steel wheels. Now, prematurely, it is at the end of its life as nobody told me ball bearings had to be kept greased. The sea is best early in the morning. I go for a swim as soon as I get up from my camp bed on the balcony: the water is absolutely still and transparent, but the sea bed is always differently moulded and ribbed according to the movement of the waters, the seaweed more, or less conspicuous, or totally vanished, the beaches empty of the monstrous crowds that will soon invade them, and the only signs of life are little fishing boats on the horizon sailing out of the Arab port of Jaffa. Occasionally, the sea washes up crates of tinned meat and strange indistinguishable ragged objects floating just below the surface, which might be the remains of sailors lost at sea. Only during December does the sea become menacingly grey, roaring with white-foaming waves that crash on the promenade, while the wind whistles through the tattered awnings of the now abandoned terraces of fashionable cafés. The sea is a constant presence, not least because it acts as a disinfectant and healer of the frequent cuts and abrasions one sustains while running barefoot in shorts, often under attack from hostile gangs of youths.

I now have a long trek to the Polish school in Montefiore Street. Outside the gates at breaktime Arab ice-cream vendors bawl out Polish obscenities in the mistaken belief acquired from the schoolchildren that these words describe the colours and flavours of their wares. The school functions six days a week, and as I march there on a Sabbath with my prominent school satchel, I get stoned by Jewish children. I have already heard of anti-Jewish pogroms in Central Europe and I can understand the irony of the situation. In the streets leading to the school pitched battles erupt between Jewish youths and Polish schoolchildren, reinforced by youngsters from a nearby Polish military college. Several local schools have to be closed for the duration. I had assumed the cause of this hostility of Jews towards non-Jewish Europeans was the news filtering through of German concentration camps, but my sister informs me that Jewish Soviet sympathisers, of which there were many at the time, were reacting to the anti-Soviet stories being spread by Poles freshly released from Soviet labour camps. Apparently, the police acknowledge that Polish schoolchildren were the victims of these sympathisers. Perhaps there is truth in both stories.

I don't feel deeply involved in these politico-cultural brawls, as I develop a different lifestyle on the streets of Tel Aviv, where all my companions are Hebrew-speaking Jews and I soon become fluent in the language. We play various street games from cops-and-robbers to the more refined games with marbles and cubes of mosaic stone (or marble, if we are lucky or rich). The marbles come in all sizes and colours: the big transparent ones with a magical flower-like pattern embedded in their centres are the most coveted. But the cube game is more intricate, more sophisticated, requiring great concentration and agility. There are five cubes the size of large dice. You throw them on the ground, you pick one up and throw it in the air; while it is falling you scoop one of the four remaining ones and turn your palm to catch the one that is falling. You then have to scoop two together, eventually all four. This is only the first stage. This game is refined also in this sense: if you lose, you simply lose the game and that is that, as in chess; whereas when you lose in marbles, your stock of marbles begins to diminish, just as you lose chips in roulette. (Those who cannot afford marbles have to make do with beer-bottle tops.) Hence, tempers can get more frayed. There is a lot of shouting and if that happens during the siesta, blinds rattle upwards and elderly hands tip buckets of water over the pitch and our heads. And if my luck holds too long, my Jewish friends suddenly remember my alien provenance: they draw crosses in the sand and spit on them. I am at a considerable disadvantage because the Star of David takes longer to draw. Moreover, they can simply cross their index fingers for the desired effect, whereas no finger contortions can produce a star.

We live in the street also because all the good food is to be got there. At the corner of Frishman and Ben Yehuda under the shade of several leafy trees you can always buy iced cactus fruit from a stall vendor. The fruit ready to be sold lies in melting ice blocks which are supplied by horse-drawn cold-boxes. Other delicacies usually available include hot corn on the cob, freshly pressed orange juice, sticks of sugarcane, watermelon and spicy meatballs tucked into Arab loaves like sachets. Some of this conspicuous consumption is financed from flower deliveries on the Jewish New Year, but mostly by grants from my mother's purse and from winnings. We also have our own gourmet recipe: you steal a large potato which you then half-bury in petrol-soaked sand and set it alight. When you bite the charred remnant, your taste buds experience a symphony of delights: burnt skin, rawish potato flesh with a distinct petrol flavour. When we have feasted sufficiently, we move onto an empty building plot, with a tall brick wall at one end, which we use for our peeing contest: who can pee highest? It is understood that girls are at a disadvantage and are not expected to compete. Other pastimes include stealing goldfish from ponds, deflating bicycle tyres, climbing tall trees in search of sweet green fruit resembling blackberries in shape (were they mulberries?), smashing the large windows of a newly furbished shop in Hajarkon.

I exchange a sackful of marbles for an excellent, wire-framed catapult, but Tuki seizes it from me as I take aim at a passer-by from behind a hedge. Tuki is the respected elder boy in the locality, whose actions and edicts we feel obliged to acknowledge. My great unfulfilled ambition is to acquire a knuckleduster, not just a clumsy leaden home-made job but the real thing in shiny metal. I would then be totally safe from bullies and other gangs.

Those of us who are ideologically more mature throw stink bombs into Pani Zatorska's flat in the villa next to ours. She is a tiny woman, with a kindly face and a receding husband, who sways alarmingly on her elephantine hips. She teaches in the Polish school and is well-known for her communist sympathies.

The gutter too yields rich treasures: cigarette butts and brightly coloured Navy Cut cigarette cartons with tiny pictures of ships, which you can cut out and use to play at table-top naval battles. One day I bring home a condom which I fill up with water from the bathroom tap: it expands and distends unbelievably and doesn't burst. Just then father enters and all hell is let loose. He also catches me smoking and I lose the taste for this pastime for good.

My Polish friend Kazik is an expert in organising mayhem in our flat when the rest of the family is away. My parents observe bitterly that he would never do that in his divorced mother's neat little apartment a few blocks away. But he is a clever lad and has already written his first novel, so I plan to write mine on the theme: In time of war should we first save works of art or people? He is my 'best friend' and after the period of our teenage adventures we shall meet again briefly in London during our student days, before he finally disappears from my life to reside with a countess in a castle in Spain.

The novel-writing phase passes quickly and I am inexorably turning into the sort of boy my parents wouldn't want me to play with. So Zosia tries to interest me in reading. There is a Jewish library tucked somewhere behind Allenby near the Migdal Or cinema, which lends pre-war Polish books. Most of these are in tatters, with pages missing, or brown and flaking. Old Shatterhand's amazing exploits among American Indians in Karl May's wonderful stories are therefore often inconclusive. And how did Jules Verne's hero confront his final ordeal in darkest Belgian Congo? I still don't know. The heroic tale of plucky little Boers taking on the British Empire, embellished with pictures, is almost complete. But these are desperate ad hoc measures: a more drastic remedy must be found to tame me.

For this task the Church is ready. I am being prepared for my first communion through a series of terrifying and humiliating confession exercises. I am privileged to make my first communion in Jerusalem, dressed in a white sailor's uniform and (for lack of more suitable footwear) white ballet shoes with the prescribed thin soles which wear through by the time we reach the Polish church. We also visit the various shrines but in the Last Supper Room the Muslim attendant protests vociferously when we try to pray. Our priest, ready for martyrdom, orders us to our knees. In the streets the atmosphere is tense because Jewish terrorists have just blown up the King David Hotel.

There is an air raid shelter facing our flat, abutting the garden of the twin villa opposite. We use it only once, the night when there is thunderous firing in the distance. It was reputedly a German submarine firing at the coast to the north of Tel Aviv. When Rommel gets close to Egypt there is considerable anxiety, but otherwise the war seems far away, despite the soldiers one sees everywhere, despite the blocked street-level entrance to our villa. The concrete wall proves its nuisance value when mother hires a piano and it has to be hauled through the upper storey staircase window, precariously balanced on wooden planks.

Mother is happiest playing the piano. She hopes one of us will be a Paderewski. Zosia's chances are minimal, given her preference for Polish folk melodies and dance tunes with a strong beat, so all hopes are focused on me, as I listen attentively to mother playing Bach's Inventions or her great favourite, Chopin's D flat Nocturne. But the grand family occasions occur when mother accompanies father's singing. In his mellow, expressive baritone he performs Fauré's sacred songs, Karłowicz's pieśni, Italian operatic arias and Tosti's

Neapolitan melodies. Mother often comments that we would have been so much better off had he taken up singing instead of social work, politics and commerce.

For we are very poor. Mother's fragmentary diary for this period reiterates phrases like: 'There is no money and there is nothing to sell' and, 'Materially things are deteriorating and the end of the war is not in sight.' As veteran of Marshal Piłsudski's First World War Legions who had remained fiercely loyal to the old charismatic leader throughout the independence years, father is out of favour with the new Government-in-Exile in London under General Sikorski, the Marshal's one-time protégé but now a bitter enemy of his loyalists.

So father is not allowed into the army and we have to make do with assistance from the Polish social services. With time on his hands, he works on a tobacco blend agreeable to the palate of Polish troops and designs a board game based on the map of Europe, with Polish soldiers fighting their way to Warsaw on every front. In exchange for a subsidy from the Polish Red Cross, he offers the sales proceeds to aid Polish war-wounded, but somehow the project flounders. He also involves himself in vociferous anti-communist politics. This is probably why he is beaten up one night as he emerges from a friend's flat and staggers home in the early hours with blood pouring from his head. He is given first-aid by Zosia, our budding medical expert, who has already gained considerable experience from attending to my frequent wounds and bruises. Soon afterwards a slow-moving black limousine pushes me from behind with its wide bumper as I balance on a kerb of an unmade pavement – and speeds away. Then mother is beaten up in broad daylight, her hands full with our hot lunch, which she is carrying all the way from a Polish soup kitchen somewhere near Allenby Boulevard. Her assailant is apparently a mad woman. Home early from school that day and waiting for mother in the street, I watch the scene helplessly from a distance on a strangely deserted noonday Hajarkon.

Random memories

Mother has decorated the 'music' room walls with exotic art-nouveau flowers.

The living-room table has a glass top covering an assortment of maps which aid discussions on the war situation.

Cooking is done on a very slick table-top Czech cooker. It runs on paraffin which tends to leak and engulf the cooker in flames.

When I am forced to obey the siesta rules, my friends call out from below 'Eifo Adam?' [Where is Adam?] and father is amused.

A Scots Regiment bagpiper breaks the siesta rules and plunges into a melancholy drone on a deserted shimmering street.

Pan Niwerżański, a Polish Jew, delivers groceries from a large round wicker basket and discusses politics: he inclines to the generally shared view that the war will not last long and we shall soon be on our way home.

CHAPTER 8

The French connection

(1943–1944)

One Sunday morning a Jewish cellist and a Jewish violinist join father for a rehearsal in the flat and then we all travel to Jaffa, where father is to sing solo at St Peter's Church during a Polish commemorative mass. This is a doctrinal triumph for him, as the Church doesn't encourage individuals to show off in holy places, and it's not the first time he has tried to have his way.

The dusty main thoroughfare in dingy, squalid, dilapidated Jaffa, is teeming with beggars and cripples, the air pungent and heavy with spices and sinuous, plaintive oriental music, blaring from shops. The Polish pilgrims are tempted by rows of Arab street vendors, who scoop sculptures of fly-blown pistachio ice-cream from large churns. As I listen to father's voice effortlessly filling the bright, cavernous vaults of the church, I don't yet know that within days I shall be commuting to the bus terminal outside the monumental and forbidding prison in the heart of Jaffa, which we have just passed, to attend the French Collège St Joseph.

It is on the way back from church that father casually

announces that my days in the Polish school are over and that I am being transferred to the Catholic monastic establishment with immediate effect, principally to gain fluency in foreign languages. The suddenness of this decision, combined with the realisation that I shall be plunged into a totally strange school environment in the centre of Jaffa, leaves me in a state of shock and apprehension.

So now I am in a class of sixty-five Arabs in black tunics with white round collars, who keep asking me 'Where is Eve?' I cringe at the thought of being dressed like a girl and luckily I am allowed to wear ordinary clothes: the idea of making my way to school in this quaint effeminate garb through swinging Tel Aviv is too embarrassing even to contemplate. But did mother during my difficult and painful birth hope for a girl and did she, like Sophie Rilke, try to maintain an illusion for as long as possible ? Before the war my curly hair was grown long, my blouses were at times distastefully frilly, my interest in dolls was encouraged, and only recently I am given a pair of mother's discarded pink silk knickers and low-heeled shoes to wear: during a game of football with my local gang, the silk begins to slip and that concentrates their attention on my funny shoes which (to add injury to insult and humiliation) pinch as well.

But maybe the explanation is much simpler. Maybe it's all a consequence of our wretched poverty, which is why perhaps I am also made to wear clothes made out of bits of father's old discarded greenish-black three-piece suit and at least one pair of my new shoes turns out to have heels stuffed with newsprint. I become aware how others live when we visit friends in the outer suburb who have two agreeable sons somewhat older than me. They reside in a vast modern flat with picture windows and ingenious gadgets in a block which overlooks the deserts beyond. To add to my unease, mother always insists that I eat well before these visits, so that I don't display unseemly greed at supper. This family shared father's exile in Romania. The elder son will die storming Monte Cassino with the Polish II Corps and the younger will turn out to be mentally retarded.

To reach my new school, I catch a Jewish bus along Ben Yehuda, the ultra-modern No.4 with plush seats and doors that shut automatically with a huff and a hiss. In the centre of Tel Aviv, off Allenby, I transfer to an olive-green Arab bus, which takes me along ruinous, twisting, narrow streets to the heart of Jaffa. This bus is usually crowded with Arab women wrapped in black from top to toe. When I chivalrously give up my seat, they sit me on their knees and I feel deeply embarrassed. At the terminal I still have a long walk uphill.

Collège St Joseph is a massive Escorial-type edifice, separated by a high wall from its twin girls' school, where the uniform is a bright red-and-white check pinafore. At school we sit alphabetically in rows of primitive black, scratched benches. I sit towards the back, because I am twenty-second on the register after all the Abd-el Kassims and the Abu Hassans. You have to be alert during roll-call. Teacher doesn't call out the names on the register. He may call the first name to set the process in train, then you have to ensure that you answer with your 'present' at the right moment. Moreover, you have to check whether the boy just above you on the register is present. If not, you have to call, 'Abu Hassan absent – present.' Wrapped in a gown, teacher sits on an elevated podium, menacingly swishing his cane. The glass-framed door behind him leads to a long corridor which runs through the length of the school. The door at the other end of the classroom leads to the playground, the row of windows on our right overlooks another part of the playground. Lessons begin with prayers in French and end in mid afternoon with prayers in French. In between we are taught mathematics, English, Arabic and French which includes a lot of learning by rote: say a new Lafontaine poem or a medium-length prayer to be learnt by the following morning.

For mathematics we have tiny books bound in navy-blue flexible covers with a reinforced spine in black. The cover bears inscriptions in black which is hardly legible against the blue. Inside there are columns of figures, exercises in the basic four mathematical operations. We spend hours multiplying figures like 1,389,782 x 3,782,999 or dividing 7,447,824 by 3,777,999. English is taught by a small man in a brownish-grey suit. He brandishes a short, thick bamboo cane which he uses with great effect as and when necessary, quite often in fact. If offered a caning, you have to come out to the front, unless you are there already, summoned because you are unable to make sense of teacher's questions, and receive a beating on your palms. If after a few strokes you begin to nurse your palms under your armpits too readily and persistently, teacher begins to use the cane indiscriminately on other parts of your anatomy.

One subject the Arab boys don't have to be taught is trade. I lose (or is it stolen?) a beautiful fountain pen, a gift from my parents, during a morning class. When teacher tries to trace its whereabouts an hour or so later, he discovers that it has already changed hands a dozen times.

The initial religious and administrative manoeuvres complete, we file out of the classroom to the chapel on an upper floor: an airy baroque creation in the heart of the school. Apart from the priest who celebrates mass for us every day, there are the other friars in black habits who haunt the endless corridors and staircases or are seen supervising the ultimate punishment: a line of pupils, heads bowed over a book from which they have to memorise passages, are made to march slowly in circles round the courtyard in the blazing sun, while a benign minister of Christ watches from a shady colonnade. Van Gogh's celebrated etching of prisoners exercising in the yard well illustrates the spirit of this pedagogic enterprise. When one of the reverend fathers suddenly dies, our prayers for his soul rise joyfully out of the routinely pious murmurs.

At the far end of the playground, hidden behind the colonnade, is a lower form where I go for my lessons in Arabic and I am keen to master the beautiful and complicated script under the guidance of an enthusiastic and sympathetic teacher. In this school Polish is useless and Hebrew positively dangerous — the incentive to improve on my English and learn French and Arabic is therefore very strong.

The school functions seven days a week, with half-days on Wednesdays and Sundays. A holiday spirit pervades the Sunday sessions: a longer than usual mass, followed by a Charlie Chaplin film, followed by an art lesson: teacher produces a very long ruler from his desk and with a few master strokes on the black-board creates an image of a ship. We in turn use our rulers to copy the image into our drawing pads. Ernst Gombrich's *Art and Illusion* contains a photograph of a Victorian classroom with similar serried ranks of black-tunicked children copying an image of a leaf a teacher has drawn on the blackboard, seemingly without a ruler.

At the end of the school day I run downhill to the bus

station, stopping briefly in an aromatic grocery shop where father has arranged for me to have a drink of a cool Arabic beverage. But there are days when I cannot face the joys of the French education system any more. I spend them on the Tel Aviv beach instead, where I build castles for Biba Hulanicka, but this romance does not last. Her father works for British Intelligence and is duly blown up by terrorists. On those days I am careful not to return home too early, but it is perhaps my relaxed countenance and my inability to give a coherent picture of the day's schooling that eventually enables my sneaky sister to rumble me. I get whipped ignominiously on my bare legs with Rozetka's leather lead and am asked to account for my unused bus fares. I have been giving them away to the cripples that line the Jaffa streets: this explanation is met with cynical jeers and I have to nurse my pain and resentment in silence.

These escapades finally convince father that I should be moved to another school (Zosia later claims credit for persuading him). I plead that if I must be in a foreign school, let it be the English St George's in Jaffa, of which I had heard good reports from a Polish pupil there. I leave St Joseph clutching my annual report (a cardboard folder full of figures in black and red, like a giant multiplication table) and a special gift from the Fathers handed to me at the end-of-year ceremony. The gift is a French illustrated book showing the world conquests of French missionary Catholicism. There are pictures of converted African lepers and other exotic peoples and diagrams showing the satisfying preponderance of Catholics over all other believers.

CHAPTER 9

The British connection

(1944–1945)

St George's in Jaffa, run by Mr Cook and his wife, who both take us for lessons in English language and literature, is a delight, even though soon after my arrival, Mr Cook gives me six of the best with a bamboo cane for my uncomplimentary description in Arabic of an Arab fellow-pupil's parentage. I escape even worse punishment by pleading plausibly, though mendaciously, that I didn't really understand what I was saying; but I lack the rhetorical skills necessary to persuade the headmaster that I acted under severe provocation from a loathsome bully.

Mr Cook is very tall and gaunt, with a long thin face and hollow cheeks, to be seen during assemblies dressed in a light grey suit and clutching a large black Bible. In the interest of complementarity, Mrs Cook is half his size, plump, with a round face and smiling eyes guarded by severe but delicate gold-framed spectacles. Her expositions of the mysteries of the English grammar and syntax are brisk, business-like and lucid. Our class of about twenty is made up of a variety of nationalities, including one English boy called David, who has neatly combed yellow hair above a neat little face, and is a favourite with some Arab teachers.

The school is at a dead end off a main street which is in no-man's-land between Tel Aviv and Jaffa; and the dusty playground overlooks a railway yard where very occasionally an antique steam engine may be heard puffing and clanking. There is also a tiny tuck shop which introduces me to the disgusting horrors of black liquorice. Unlike its grand French counterpart, this school is housed in a modest two-storey building. Not aspiring to grandeur, it also doesn't aspire to be a reformatory for juvenile delinquents: the atmosphere is relaxed and friendly, there are no black tunics, no sinister clerics.

So when one day my parents call to take me away during school hours to participate in a young musicians' competition in Tel Aviv, I am annoyed and embarrassed at this interference with school routines: and perhaps I already sense that mother is grooming me to be my generation's Paderewski, a role for which I am totally unfit, but which mother had mapped out for me with complete confidence and which she will try to make me pursue over many years to come.

I practise the piano at home and have lessons from Lili Wittenberg in her elegant villa on a leafy boulevard a considerable distance from home. I and her other pupils give a concert in March 1945 at the studio of Professor J. Ebenstein at 19 Mapu Street. Among many others, Szula Prawda plays the minuet from Mozart's *Don Giovanni*, Judith Lubelczyk and Josefa Amdurski play the *Song of the Volga Boatmen* for four hands, while I join Aliza Katz in a Polish Catholic hymn and perform solo a patriotic Polish song; but Aliza Katz is clearly the star pupil, for when she performs on her own she manages a Debussy Arabesque and a movement from a Mozart piano concerto.

I have no memory of this event at all and an examination of the tatty typewritten programme has no Proustian effect either. But it obviously seemed momentous to all concerned at the time. All three of us reported on it in a composite letter written to father who had gone to Egypt to join the army at last. Zosia wrote: 'Adam's concert was a great success; admittedly he was sweating with emotion and [said] his fingers were "sliding all over" but he hit away with verve. Today we've both been to confession, and tomorrow we go to communion. Adam is quite bearable, that is, polite, he reads books, so there is peace in the house.' And mother reports that, according to my wishes, I wore a white long-sleeved shirt and a navy-blue waistcoat; and I add a couple of sentences reminding him of the tough bargain: If I play he buys me a set of soldiers.

A big cinema in Dizengoff Square is showing *A Song to Remember* with Paul Muni playing Chopin and Rubinstein playing the music and Ava Gardner playing George Sand and drops of the sick genius's technicolour blood falling on the keyboard in the climactic final sequence. The queues are endless, all Poles are there, and there is sheet music on sale with samples of simplified nocturnes, mazurkas and polonaises. I make a thought-provoking discovery: this easy music lies awkwardly under the fingers, is therefore more difficult to play and sounds so much less impressive than the originals. The Polish community also organises theatricals, reviews shows and displays of patriotic uplift, while colossal cinema billboards in Allenby Square advertise *For Whom the Bell Tolls* and other cinematic hits of the day which include *Lady Hamilton*, where the action alternates between boring ballroom scenes and sailing ships swaying in the high seas to the sound of gunfire.

No sooner have I established myself happily at St George's when I hear the shattering news that the school is to close. After the last assembly Mr and Mrs Cook shake our hands as we file past with tears in our eyes. For the following school year we are recommended to transfer to the larger, more firmly established sister school, the St George's Boarding School in Jerusalem.

CHAPTER 10

Jerusalem

(1945–1946)

In July 1943 General Sikorski, the Head of the Polish Government-in-Exile in London, has died in a mysterious air crash on take-off from Gibraltar after a tour of Polish army units in the Middle East. The reorganised Polish Government is more sympathetic to people with Marshal Piłsudski loyalties. But the wheels grind slow and it is not until February 1945 that father is re-admitted into the army with the rank of captain. He travels to army headquarters in the exotic and mysterious city of Cairo and brings us back luxurious presents: a striped bottle-green Parker pen for mother and a pair of real-leather football boots for me: they are a size too small but for a while at least I endure the discomfort to enjoy a game with my admiring gang.

Our days in Tel Aviv are now numbered. Zosia travels to Nazareth to join the Polish Forces School of Young Female Volunteers, father gets an assignment in Beirut to look after the families of Polish military personnel in Lebanon and will leave Palestine with mother in October, while I am being got ready for Jerusalem. My parents painstakingly collect the clothing required by boarding-school rules, but even with the sudden affluence they can't afford the full outfit, and after he sends us the first consignment of luxurious presents mother warns father to be careful with money.

She also notes in her diary on 11 October: 'At last news from Poland that Janka and Kocio are alive – Jacek perished [in August the previous year] as a soldier of the Home Army — sad and painful news, so much blood!' And a week later: 'I've learnt of his death so recently – thus everything turns into nothingness but history records.'

This news reaches my parents just after father deposits me at St George's and this probably explains why it doesn't reach me till much later. Meanwhile, at the age of ten I spend my first day away from our ever changing home, wretched and lonely, as I am quick to inform father in my tear-spattered letter that evening. The first consolation is the discovery that a Jewish friend from Tel Aviv has also enrolled but we have to whisper in corners because Hebrew is banned by the school rules. Neither then, nor since, have I been able to decide whether British policy in Palestine was pro-Arab or pro-Israeli.

My other consolation is the spaghetti with tomato sauce, followed by heaps of fresh green olives, for which I and my newly found chubby genial Arab friend acquire a taste in our crypt-like basement refectory. No Italian restaurant has ever been able to match that first gourmet experience.

Arabs are the dominant group at the school, many of them from very rich families in Jordan and Egypt.

The school is a pleasant, collegiate-like complex of stone buildings overlooking Golgotha, with the Hebrew University nestling in the hills beyond, the YMCA further up the road and the new gleaming Polish House round the corner. The Old City's Damascus Gate is a short walk away past the tuck shop, the YMCA and the British Consulate. Our junior school, where we have our dormitories, refectory, classrooms and playground is divided by the road from the senior school and the neo-gothic St George's Cathedral which is also our school chapel. We cross the road for special weekly assemblies in the gym conducted by Mr Simpson, the headmaster. I stand in the front row and have a good view of his immaculately tailored suit which, to my amazement, is different every week. He is a middle-aged, middle-sized man with a round face and thinning hair and the smooth, commanding yet undramatic voice I was later to associate with British civil servants and businessmen, and unlike the more appealing, hesitant, mannered speech of Mr Cook who would have fitted well into the senior common-room of an Oxford college.

Mr Sagg, our housemaster, reads us bedtime stories in his flat above our dormitory, while we sit around in our pyjamas on little stools in a room which has a slightly nauseating bitter-sweet smell and Mrs Sagg pottering in the background. He has a tiny body, with arms and legs distorted by polio. He has nevertheless a fearsome reputation, and when he shuffles grotesquely along the main corridor and yells out commands in a strange, guttural whine, we are on our best behaviour. When he plays table-tennis in the games room, flailing and jerking his arms and dragging his feet, we know he will eventually defeat even the most agile young opponent. So I am particularly pleased when this formidable master joins a tightly-knit group of spectators crowding round me as I win at chess against the much older, cocky and bumptious dormitory prefect.

The game had hardly begun and the board is still messily cluttered with black and white pieces when I spot my chance against his suddenly exposed king and produce the classic gambit with my two rooks. Years later, in London, as I am about to board a 52 bus outside the Albert Hall, I come face to face with Mr Sagg, as he negotiates a descent from the back platform. I pass inside too stunned to say a word and then, as the bus speeds away, reflect bitterly on my indecisiveness.

Our geography master is a young ex-policeman who takes us on expeditions into Old Jerusalem, which he clearly knows well from his days on the beat; the Arab mathematics teacher introduces us to the excitements of geometry in a classroom in the senior school overlooking our playing fields. Not all the pupils are attracted to the intellectual rigours of this discipline, so from time to time he has to call out in his sad, low resonant voice: 'Please stop murmuring at the back there,' with the heavily rolled 'r' in 'murmuring', characteristic of Arab pronunciation of English. Miss Mudge is the new young teacher of English. She tells us she comes from a big Midlands city called Birmingham. At the start of each lesson she pulls out from her bag a big ticking alarm-clock and places it dramatically on top of her desk. If there is an outbreak of insubordination, she warns us to behave, folds her arms ostentatiously and stares determinately at the clock to see how long it will take us to settle down. She teaches us to recite 'Twinkle, twinkle, little star. . .'

Once a week after lessons I have musical tuition from a young Czech pianist; the evening study and homework hour in the classroom I often spend studying the classic Polish Renaissance translation of the New Testament. The reasons for this devotion are complex: as a Christian, I have to attend chapel on Sundays. As a

Catholic, I not only feel religiously persecuted, but I also resent the austerity of the Anglican Cathedral's interior and the lengthy, colourless and boring services which are not even conducted in Latin. The authentic *Nihil Obstat* version of God's message is my defence against heretical assaults on my conscience. On the other hand, the matter-of-fact historical approach to Biblical stories that St George's encourages has much more appeal than the Catholic insistence on turning every episode into a pallid symbol or tedious parable and the Church's overall preference that the flock should study approved summaries and interpretations of the holy scriptures, rather than the scriptures themselves. The ubiquitous solid presence of holy sites confirms the rightness of this direct approach and the Acts of the Apostles is a gripping adventure story by any standards.

Father comes down at Christmas and we spend a fairly bleak festive season in the marble halls of the bright but cold Polish House; snow has fallen and the steep Jerusalem pavements are slushy and slippery.

After two terms at St George's my religious scruples are resolved by events. I catch measles and infect the rest of the school, which has to close for the rest of the school year. I spend the first few days in the school sick-room and when father arrives, I am transferred to a private clinic in New Jerusalem run by nuns. I spend several weeks recovering in a darkened room. My Czech music teacher comes to visit me with a present of a huge jigsaw puzzle that saves me from hours of boredom. As I was leaving the classroom after our last lesson, she stayed behind and played Chopin's *Revolutionary Study* which gradually faded away as I walked slowly down the colonnaded passage. Years later in London, as I was preparing to take my BA exams in

Top: Marshal Piłsudski surrounded by
his officers c. 1920: father is third left,
uncle Świtalski extreme right

Above: Mother greets Marshal
Piłsudski in Žitomir; behind him stands
Gen. W. Sikorski, later prime minister

Top: Myself in the Warsaw flat c. 1939   Above: Uncle Konstanty with his sisters

Right: My sister and I

Top: Myself, Zosia and Jacek   Above: Mother and I

Left: My sister and I

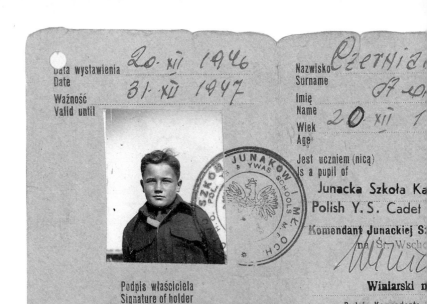

Data wystawienia 20. XII 1946
Date
Ważność 31. XII 1947
Valid until

Podpis właściciela
Signature of holder

Nazwisko CZETNIC...
Surname
Imię
Name
Wiek 20 XII 1
Age

Jest uczniem (nicą)
Is a pupil of
Junacka Szkoła Ka
Polish Y.S. Cadet
Komendant Junackiej S:
na Śr. Wscho...

Winiarski n

Podpis Komendanta
O. Cs Signatur

Top: Myself in uniform

Above: With Rozetka at aunt Janka's in
occupied Warsaw c. 1940

Right: Jacek Świtalski (1928–1944)

Top: The family in Nazareth 1947   Above: The family at Cooper's Hill
                                          c. 1948

philosophy after only one year's study, and feeling the strain of that endeavour, I once woke up early in the morning, crying quietly at the thought that I shall never see my Czech teacher again. Nor will I see St George's other teachers again. A pity since I liked the school and it seemed to like me. My Arabic, English and Science were all 'very good' and the Headmaster judged me 'A very good boy in all respects'.

CHAPTER 11

A Lebanese idyll

(1946)

The transfer to Lebanon in the spring of 1946 starts
well. In Haifa father orders a taxi to take us all the way
to Beirut. I am allowed to sit next to the driver; I am
wearing a pair of navy-blue shorts and a windcheater
of blue-and-white check. We drive along the coastal
highway through Sidon and Tyre and get out of the car
at the frontier for a passport check by French border
guards. The landscape is now more dramatic, with
cypress-covered mountain ranges on the right and the
sea on the left. This is no longer the parched landscape
of Palestine, and the settlements are ruinous, exotic
antiquities, like Jaffa, with no trace of that neat,
functional architecture which the Jewish immigrants
had introduced south of the border.

We drive to the centre of Beirut and then west from
the central square along rue Georges Picot and disembark alongside a small apartment block at 4 rue
Poste where mother is waiting for us. Here we rent
rooms from a spirited youngish widow who together
with her maturing daughter become visibly excited
whenever there is a naval visit in the port. The flat has

views over the bay and the snow-capped mountains. At some stage we move to a nearby cottage with a garden cunningly hidden up a steep alleyway off rue Georges Picot.

I am enrolled at the American International College attached to the American University, a campus of elegant, modern, honey-coloured buildings, including an observatory, scattered in woodland running along a sandy beach. The American school does not display any of the relentless educational zeal of Collège St Joseph or even the undramatic yet purposeful attitudes of the two St Georges: the timetable is light, the enticing private beach seems to be the focus of the curriculum and what is left over for classroom work is perfunctory, limited and of a standard that would have been considered too low two grades further down at St George's. Even the Grade Card is an undistinguished scrap of paper.

This schooling-as-leisure activity leaves me with lots of time to explore Beirut on foot, by bike and, above all, riding the three tram routes, which stretch right across the city, and converge in the central square, where a lot of manual shunting takes place: standing on the open platform next to the driver, I am occasionally allowed to drag the heavy shunting rod down the steps to the shunt-point. The No. 2 tram starts way past the American University, by a beautiful sandy cove reserved for French officers where I am also allowed thanks to father's military standing. Once he takes me to lunch in the British Army Officers' Club and is nonplussed by a dessert consisting of a modest oblong of Cheddar cheese, its modesty emphasised by the large crested blue-rimmed plate it is served on.

For a twopenny flat rate the tram takes me along an elegant thoroughfare with views of the sea; after a dramatic sharp bend it descends steeply into rue Georges Picot, spewing sand along the track to assist braking down this perilous incline. The No. 3 tram starts at the central square and it soon ascends gradually south away from the coast towards leafy opulent suburbs, swaying gently as it speeds along the centre of a wide, straight boulevard. No. 1 travels to the port and the industrial district but I rarely use it. Occasionally I dare to leap onto the open platform of a moving tram; once I slip off: luckily it is the driver's platform and he brakes sharply to enable me to pick myself up and clamber on. He doesn't lecture me on safety but the lesson sinks in.

Soon after I arrive, public transport comes to a standstill for a few days. This is my first experience of a strike, this strange modern phenomenon, made even more puzzling by the simultaneous appearance of the hammer-and-sickle symbol on walls.

Here French is the common language and the city has a distinctly French feel in the look of the shops, the westernised manners of the Lebanese, the Empire-style building façades, the tree-lined boulevards, the French B-pictures, like the thrilling series about *La police contre le dragon noir* unfolding week by week in a cinema in the central square, and crunchy, tasty baguettes. I have a bicycle which I ride along the side streets until one day I am stopped by a policeman who demands to see my licence. I honestly plead total ignorance of this requirement, and as I do this in fluent Arabic, I am allowed to go free with a smile and a caution.

This encounter persuades me to do more of my exploring on foot. I find a bench in a quiet square and I sit down to read the book I brought with me. The book is thin and has a hard light-brown cover, but what is inside it? The memory is lost. More memorable is a heavy volume in light green covers, an American history of the ancient world with wonderful revelations about Greek civilisation and a picture of a bearded sage called Plato. This book makes a very brief appearance in the house and father is unable or unwilling to tell me what had happened to it: certain other books are kept on top of the cupboard away from my prying eyes. But a little slim volume in a grey-green cover is readily available: published in Edinburgh in 1943 it contains two texts by the nineteenth century Polish poet and dramatist Juliusz Słowacki: *Anhelli*, a parable about Polish exiles in Siberia and a narrative poem, a graphic tale of disease and death in an Arab family. Exiled from Poland and settled in Switzerland, Słowacki had undertaken a comprehensive tour of the Middle East, travelling to Lebanon from Egypt and Palestine, which he commemorated in *Journey to the East*, a discursive narrative poem. He had spent some months in a monastery at Beit-Chash-Ban, in the hills above Beirut. It was in the Lebanese hills that he wrote *Anhelli*, and now, a new generation of Polish exiles in Lebanon, led by my father, has honoured the poet with a plaque in the ruined retreat. Hence the appearance in the flat of the Edinburgh edition and of a leaflet commemorating the unveiling: I have them still.

Father also takes me on visits to other villages in the mountains, where many Polish families are housed. His Arab driver performs heart-stopping acrobatics on precipitous Z-bends. But the road to Damascus is smooth, wide and straight. It also happens to be wet and covered in leaves, and a Polish driver of the half-ton truck, very probably under the influence of alcohol (although my sister, a firm believer in the integrity of Polish non-commissioned officers, denies this at a subsequent enquiry) loses control in a skid and we are scattered on the tarmac and in the ditch. We, that is a group of us sitting on little benches along the sides of the back of the truck: the driver and my sister who is sitting next to him, remain unharmed in the cab. I recover fairly easily from the ditch, but I see father lying on his back in the middle of the road, moaning. I notice that my scout-belt, a recent proud purchase, is undone. It must have caught against something as I was being flung out from the back of the truck, slowing my progress and thus diminishing the severity of my head wound: an early example of the utility of seat belts. We return to Beirut by ambulance, concussed, bleeding and bruised. The worst is a state of shock, from which I take months to recover. Initially I am afraid to walk along the streets, where the heavy rumble of my beloved trams is now the cause of distress and even panic, and I divert into side streets whenever I can; while car journeys are a source of deep anxiety, especially after a trip during which I spot a military vehicle lying on its side by the coastal road south of Beirut. Nobody thinks of treating me for shock: perhaps such treatment wasn't fashionable in those days.

The Poles, betrayed by the Allies at Yalta and excluded even from victory parades, remain bitter and desperate. By a bizarre coincidence only the Lebanese government, along with the Vatican, the Irish Republic and Cuba, continues to recognise the Polish Government-in-Exile and so the Polish non-communist flag, with a crowned eagle in the middle, is still guarding the Polish consulate in Beirut. The French are likely to pull out of Lebanon; the British, increasingly battered by Jewish and Arab terrorists, are likely to pull out of Palestine. Polish communists, anxious that as many Polish soldiers as possible should return to Stalin's Poland and legitimise it, are spreading rumours about the awful fate that awaits us all in England as internees and coal miners. Newsreels of snow-bound austerity Britain offer further encouragement. The fate of civilians may be worse, so father decrees I should be in uniform. One evening he tells me that the following morning at dawn I am to mount a Polish army truck bound for the Polish cadet camp deep in the Palestinian desert towards Gaza. Terrified, I cry all night. The Lebanese idyll is at an end and I shall never improve on my French: the additional six months I reckon I need for fluency eludes me at a critical moment.

It's 18 September 1946 and mother notes in her diary: 'Today Adam departed to the cadet camp. He was very frightened. There is emptiness and sadness.'

Within a couple of weeks my parents too are on the move – to Nazareth. They leave behind Rozetka – recently dead – in a Beirut cemetery.

CHAPTER 12

Army days

(September 1946 – October 1947)

I have to catch the truck at dawn and the three of us – the driver and another soldier and I – make our way back to Palestine along the coastal road through Haifa. Somewhere along the way we have breakfast at a roadside inn and I get my first taste of beer – remembering father's way with alcohol, I down the glass rapidly on an empty stomach and a swimming sensation in my head lasts for several hours. We reach Jerusalem in the evening and then drive on to Emmaus. As I walk there with these two strange men in uniform towards our quarters I reflect, not for the first time in this land, on the fusion of the legendary-biblical with the contemporary random insignificant events in which I participate.

In the morning we drive back through the hills on the Jerusalem-Tel Aviv highway, trailing billows of smoke. The driver of an overtaking British army light truck alerts us to our defective brakes. Did we get out and conclude our journey in the next Polish military truck that came along? That would seem reasonable and I have this image in my mind of seeing our truck from a distance parked at the side of the road. I am inclined to trust the memory image even though it took me a while in reflection to draw the right conclusion from it.

We now drive south to the northern edge of the desert, the vegetation, mainly cactus, is sparse, and usually signals the presence of a Bedouin encampment of black tents and camels; there are also mud-coloured police forts set back from the main road. At midday we arrive at Barbara Camp shimmering in the sun some miles from the sea in the hinterland of Ashkalon just north of Gaza. The main north-south highway flanks us in the west. The railway line to Egypt runs on the eastern side, the endless desert stretches south, while in the north we are bounded by an orange grove and a colossal, black water cistern on stilts. The sound of the irrigation pump, like that of a hiccoughing cuckoo, fills the air.

We disembark in the middle of a vast city of wooden barracks and tents scattered generously over the endless plain. I am assigned to No. 1 Company commanded by Captain Sygnarek, and I am taken to the quartermaster sergeant to collect the regulation uniforms, boots, socks, cutlery, blankets and various army paraphernalia, whose application is not immediately clear to me. Remembering the inadequacies of my wardrobe at St George's, I remark to the sergeant that I've never had such an abundance of clothing in my life. He is pleased at my recognition of his generosity.

Our company is quartered in rows of tents along the edge of the camp, with black-painted wooden latrines in the far distance by the perimeter fence. Because of their inconvenient situation, early morning calls of nature are often attended to in the sand just outside the tents and one could be forgiven for assuming the unexpected arrival of a monsoon season. My tent,

which houses six other boys, is at the edge of that
compound, with the desert beyond. We are also the
youngest in the company, pupils in the first form of the
secondary school. Way beyond, towards the perimeter
fence by the laundry, are the juniors, who are easily
recognised, because they have to button their trousers
either just below or just above their heads and forage
caps sit heavily on their ears: British Army uniforms
were not designed to fit Polish youngsters emaciated
and stunted in their growth by several years' experience
of Soviet labour camps. The standard uniform consists,
sensibly enough, of light short khaki trousers, a short-
sleeved shirt and a forage cap: long trousers and ties
are reserved for special occasions. However, we are
also obliged to wear black lace-up boots over thick
woollen socks: at night, permeated with congealed
sweat, the socks stink and stand as rigid as the boots:
luckily our tent is not sealed air-tight for draughts. This
also means that it is no defence against sandstorms:
whirling sky-high sheets of fine, hot desert sands blow
menacingly towards us from the south.

The tents have flagstone floors and the canvas is
supported by two bamboo poles. The beds have straw
mattresses slung on wooden slats, supported on wooden
stilts. A gentle but determined kick aimed at the bottom
of the bed will cause it to collapse, a very unfortunate
state of affairs for the victim, if this happens just before
sergeant's morning inspection. He expects the blankets
to form a neat, sharp-edged rectangle over the bed. A
worse and more wilfully perpetrated disaster is a 'pilot',
when a gang of older boys pulls your bed to pieces,
scattering the bedding all over the place and disturbing
the lice beneath your pillow.

The other boys in the tent are a friendly bunch, but
see me as a pampered outsider: I have a Varsovian

accent (in due course my family will tease me for my sing-song Lvovian accent, as they had earlier laughed at my Jewish intonations); I use such posh words as 'pled' [plaid] when referring to army blankets ('koce'), and 'palto' (cf. French 'paltot') instead of 'płaszcz' [coat]; I have an officer for a father – more importantly, I have a father, which is more than most of my friends can boast, and I have not seen the inside of a labour camp; most conspicuously, I am not partial to the rich ramifications of Russo-Polish foul language. Only one of them appears totally unscarred by the brutalities of his experiences in the Peoples' Paradise, and his example is my first early lesson that the Marxist principle Being Defines Consciousness is false.

Every morning after roll-call, which includes the singing of the traditional Polish morning sacred hymn which I played at that historic concert in Tel Aviv, and breakfast in a nearby hut (as we rush in, the jokers call out: 'Don't crush the lieutenant!' as he desperately attempts to form us into an orderly queue), we march to a group of huts enclosing two sides of a largish square, which is some way away from our site. One of them is our classroom.

A smart young man teaches us English: he puts on his best English accent when addressing me: he frequently uses me as a guinea-pig and example to others and calls me 'The Englishman' which doesn't do my reputation any good. A mild-mannered, sweaty middle-aged man with a soft Lithuanian accent desperately tries to teach us singing, as he blows into a silver miniature version of Pan's pipes which he keeps in the top pocket of his battle dress. A youngish woman teaches Polish literature and grammar and has to make sure that when she sits down, her knees are very close together and her tight skirt is firmly pulled down. Our literary material

includes Polish poetry, stories about classical Greece
and Kipling's *Jungle Book*.

A genial poet takes us for geography and pretends to
be embarrassed as he details, on a large map of the
Middle East, numerous place names which, in Polish,
stand for a significant part of the male anatomy. He is
clearly one of us: when a pupil is called out to locate the
Dead Sea or the Arabian Peninsula on the map next to
the blackboard, he quickly parries the attack by asking
Professor Legeżyński, affectionately known as 'Funio',
how he judges Rita Hayworth's latest picture. The
professor's fleshy face registers a dreamy smile as he
launches, with a beguiling, Lvovian lilt, into a lengthy
discourse on the lady's visible talents, until the bell cuts
him short. Years later in London he will tell me: 'I tried
to secure a poetry prize for you at the Writers' Union,
but they are all against you.' Latin is taught by a
sinister-looking, short-sighted individual called Dyrkacz,
who spits a lot in his passion to convince us of the
greatness of Classical culture. An admirable teacher
wasting his talents on us.

Although we are ultimately under British command,
the school retains its Polish traditions, so mercifully we
have no organised games. But what we miss in sport,
we make up in drill and discipline. Boots are regularly
polished, trousers are pressed (stretched damp on the
planks on which the mattress rests); there are inspec-
tions and Sunday parades. Here it is No. 4 and No. 5
Company which have mastered the art: their drill is
thrillingly faultless, especially at commemorative
night-time parades, when they march with blazing
torches (petrol-filled tin cans attached to the bayonets
of their rifles) singing the stirring yet melancholy Polish
songs.

There is also guard duty, though humiliatingly,

without loaded guns for us youngsters in No. 1 Company, while the older boys set up observation posts with live ammunition. My first assignment is to guard the kitchen cauldrons against poisoning by Arabs during the first watch which ends at 22.00 hours. The kitchens are in the middle of the camp yet isolated. But no one comes to relieve me, and I am still there at 6.00, into the third watch. I stagger back to my tent in time for the reveille.

My unprecedented devotion to duty impresses Company Commander Captain Sygnarek and he says so in the order of the day. This episode, probably reinforced by my middle-class background, decides him to appoint me in charge of the platoon. But I am by no means a charismatic leader and my duties consist mainly of taking the tent's washing to the laundry and making sure the beds are properly made each morning. My outstanding sense of responsibility is not seen as a mandatory example. When I am woken in the night by an Arab face staring at me and then swiftly vanishing into the darkness, I conclude that something has again gone wrong with the watch.

Still, our moral well-being is not neglected. In addition to classes in Catholic misinterpretations of the Old Testament, we have special meetings in the cinema (the chapel is too small for the compulsorily faithful) where the priest directs our thoughts to the unending iniquities of the Jews. The holy man provides us with incontrovertible evidence both of the Jews' malevolence and of God's omnipotence and justice. For example, earlier this century a group of Kraków Jews had conspired to steal the holy sacrament from a local church. The wicked infidels enter the church at night, seize the sacrament and take it to their repulsive basement lodgings in a block of flats. They empty the chalice onto

the table and stab the holy wafers with long pins –
when, behold! jets of blood issue from the tormented
wafers and the unspeakable criminals flee in terror.
But the blood clings to their clothes and they are soon
apprehended and punished.

The one Catholic ritual which appeals to me is the
series of May evening services in the chapel in honour
of the Virgin. The chapel is full of incense and flickering
candles and of the hypnotic incantations to Mary,
Mother of God, Tower of Ivory, Queen of Heaven,
Queen of Poland. . . The unending string of bizarre
appellations fascinate with their wild incongruity.

Next to the chapel is the library. On one of my early
visits there I come against a hostility to readers which
will pursue me all the way to the British Library.
Having devoured Bolesław Prus's *Pharaoh,* I search for
other books by him and find *The Emancipated Women.*
The librarian is most reluctant to let me have the four-
volume edition (reprinted recently in the Polish Classics
series in Jerusalem) but eventually relents and I struggle
through this tedious account of late nineteenth-century
blue-stockings, who deliver long speeches on women's
rights, the universe and everything.

In class we sit alphabetically and I share a desk with
Henryk Czerwiński. Our names are close enough to
cause confusion, even in the mind of the most alert
teacher, and we have a pact that whichever of us is
called, the one who actually knows what to say (usually
me) gets up to answer. For Henryk's intelligence resides
in his hands rather than his head, even though we
shared a surreptitious reading of Prus's gripping novel
about ancient Egypt, which we hid under the desk. As
he sits next to the wall, he carves deep with his pen-
knife into the supporting wooden beam to create a
secret strong-box protected by a metal shutter. His

particular passion is the manufacture of guns: he collects spent shells, mounts them on wooden holders, secures them with thick wire and fills them with powder ground from matchsticks. One afternoon there is an explosion in the neighbouring tent where Henryk lives. As I rush out, I see him running, clutching his hand, obviously in pain. One of his pistols lies, blackened, on the ground. He is rushed to hospital with apparently minor injuries, but puzzlingly he never returns and my one attempt to visit him in hospital fails.

R. is another boy I am fairly friendly with, but he is seduced by our welfare-officer and consequently removed from camp ignominiously for seducing the welfare-officer, who continues his habit of taking photographs of selected boys and then inviting them to his quarters to show them the results.

For more orthodox entertainment there is the ugly brick cinema which doubles as a general-purposes hall. The black-and-white pictures are flanked by sub-titles, or rather side-titles: Hebrew on the left, Polish on the right. They are hand-scratched in black on a yellowish scroll operated manually from the projection room. It requires outstanding vigilance to keep one of them synchronised with the picture, it is well-nigh impossible to keep track of both of them. So Rita Hayworth may be simultaneously saying: 'Darling, will you be my wife?' and 'Me Big Chief no like White Man'.

Army snaps

Father sends me a postal order for ten shillings. I walk to the distant post office in the midday heat to cash it. Apparently I sign in the wrong place and the friendly postmaster makes me copy out in full the small print on the back of the order before he agrees to release the money.

A trip is organised to Cairo and the Pyramids but I decline to go, fearing I shall fail my exams. A decision of intense and misguided conscientiousness which I shall bitterly regret. Learning that father has taken my sister, who has no interest in ancient history or archeology, on a visit to Baalbeck, increases the chagrin.

With more sense I resist going on a trip to the Tel Aviv Zoo. I hate seeing caged animals and, to my surprise, the officer in charge of the expedition allows me to stay behind on the excuse that, as an old Tel Aviv hand, I have seen it all already.

On my first leave I travel in a Polish Army truck to Nazareth. My parents now live here in a small Arab house with a walled garden; several monastic buildings in the centre and on the overlooking hill have been converted into Polish army schools. Father teaches business studies in one of them. Zosia has a room in another: it is full of English phrase books and dictionaries, as she now hopes to study medicine in England and her current boyfriend is a British Army sergeant called George. With a group of army friends he takes us to Lake Tiberias for a swim; we race at heart-stopping speed in a small truck, the soldiers' submachine guns at the ready. On the way back to camp from Nazareth I hitch-hike with an Army friend. It is inevitably a zig-zag route, embracing Haifa and other out-of-the-way places. We are usually picked up by allied military trucks; occasionally by Arab lorries, whose drivers I try to impress with my Arabic and encourage them to deviate from their routes. It takes all day to reach Barbara Camp but it is an exciting adventure and I have a sense of achievement.

A theatrical tour de force

It had never occurred to me, but apparently I can sing. Our silver-piping Pan from Wilno had thus reported on me, my friend Marek Schwetz and a few others. We are to act in a play – as schoolboys coming on at the end of the piece to greet the hero with song. The setting is the period leading up to Poland's independence after the First World War, the hero is Marshal Piłsudski in charge of the conquering Polish Legions. But the most important aspect of the play is the fact that after our crowd-pulling performances, we go on tour of various Polish centres and camps: Jerusalem, Tel Aviv, Nazareth, Port Said, El Qantara. . .

In Tel Aviv we lunch at the NAAFI in Hajarkon, where as a member of the armed forces, I can now enter quite legitimately. Our trucks are ranged across the road in the parking lot next to my old home. I have a chance to wander about and members of my old gang soon gather round to examine me and my uniform. But our conversation is now halting and incoherent: I realise with shock that my fluency in Hebrew has gone.

The most exciting part of the tour is the visit to Egypt. The train travels along an endless desert, when suddenly, at sunset, there is a mirage: large ocean-going ships appear steaming across the sands in front of us. On closer inspection they prove to be gliding along the Suez Canal. Soon we disembark for our quarters near the Canal. There is time to explore before our next performance, so I decide to test my sporting skills acquired in Tel Aviv: I plunge into the waters and swim across to the African side. Once on the far side, and with large ships again appearing after a brief lull, churning past at frequent intervals, I realise the enormity of my escapade. At last there is another short break in the traffic and I chance it. People wave to me from a ship that is not too far away as I struggle to the Asiatic side. Even today, this memory fills me with horror.

We visit Port Said, where the dirty-postcards merchants are busy along the quay. Excitement at the prospect of visiting Cairo is quickly quashed as we learn of a recent order making it out of bounds to military personnel. We drive back from Port Said to another camp along a narrow sweet-water canal running parallel to the main canal, in an oppressive, clammy heat, smelling of brackish water. On the way we stop at El Qantara, an amazing cool oasis of lush greenery and elegant houses. That night we perform in the main Polish camp along the Canal. Another sold-out performance. The following morning I wake to a strange sensation: there is soft music all around me. The camp is wired-up with loudspeakers. Muzak has arrived.

At Egyptian railway stations our train is well-guarded. Egyptian boys have a habit of rushing into compartments and snatching things from the racks. Nor is one safe when the train is on the move, particularly at night. They travel with us on the roof and from time to time a little hand will appear at the upper end of the window trying its luck. Egypt seems a far cry from Lebanon.

CHAPTER 13

Embarkation

(August 1947)

Soon we shall be travelling to Egypt again. . .

This time it will be the big voyage. . . We shall be sailing to England.

The summer vacations I spend with my parents in Nazareth, though father is now frequently away on army assignments at headquarters in Egypt. There isn't much to do in that remote provincial town; I tend to get on mother's nerves, especially since she too doesn't find Nazareth all that enthralling. But as she is not given to disciplining me, I eventually decide to punish myself by destroying my fine collection of mainly Polish and American stamps. However, events are now moving fast: departure to England appears imminent so I am forced to return to base, but to my chagrin much too early, as this letter which I wrote to mother on 21 July makes clear:

> I have arrived safely at Barbara Camp. We were chased out of Nazareth because the Girl Volunteers were packing. [My company friend] Schwetz didn't go because his doctor fixed it; if Daddy

were here I too could have stayed. As it is I am
stuck here and have to perform guard and other
duties every three days. It appears we won't be
leaving till the middle of August. I am very sorry
I came back when I needn't have. I don't want to
be in England on my own so try to come because
I am afraid to be there alone, and I don't want to
remain there with the Cadets. Send me George's
[Zosia's boyfriend's] address and maybe someone
else's. Do try to come to England with me
because I don't want to work in a mine. Please
cheer me up!

My hunch is correct: we are to depart in August. We
have to squeeze all our belongings into a backpack and
a big army-issue white sack like a roller, secured at the
top with a length of rope through large eyelets, reinforced with brass rings. The library is being disbanded
and I would like to fill the whole sack with books, but in
the end I have to make do with Chrzanowski's *Literature
of Independent Poland.* Someone tells me that a local
Arab photographer is giving away piles of photographs
he has taken in the camp over the years. There is a very
good one of me at a ceremony admitting me to full
cadet status, with the commanding officer securing the
yellow-lined blue epaulettes on my shoulders. I immediately send it via the Field Post to my mother, who is now
languishing in a transit camp in Ramallah, near
Jerusalem. Not surprisingly, given the general destabi-
lisation, it never reaches its destination.

A colossal, steam-belching train has stopped on open
ground outside the camp perimeter, next to the latrines,
and the whole force, with sacks and kit-bags, boards it. I
am in danger of being left behind, because sergeant
misses me out during roll-call: my name is lost in the

crease of his list and only an urgent representation on my part restores me to official existence.

The tents have all been collapsed and rolled up, leaving stranded the black water tower, some wooden huts and the monstrous brick cinema. It's a disturbing, desolate scene, as if a hurricane had devastated a city. The train pulls away across the desert. It stops once or twice at little halts. Arab boys appear from sand dunes and call out in Polish that they have boiled eggs for sale. These threaten to be my only sustenance, because almost as soon as we have boarded the train, someone steals my cutlery, so meals are tricky until a compassionate soul finds me another set.

We arrive in Port Said. On the waterfront General Wiatr, Commander-in-Chief Polish Land Forces, makes a speech. He is a tiny man lost in the crowd, which in its enthusiasm to see and hear him threatens to push him into the water. His name means 'wind'. As we embark on the troop-ship the *Chittral*, which has sailed up the Suez Canal full of British soldiers returning from India, Egyptians swarm around in rafts and boats, offering leather goods for sale and diving for coins which we throw at them from the decks.

As we steam across the Mediterranean, Pantellaria, Gibraltar and the Portugese coast are identified in the shimmering heat of late summer. Officially organised bets are laid on when we shall pass Gibraltar and the Captain slows down through the Straits to minimise the pay-out. Our boys while away the time playing poker for high stakes, watched by groups of bemused British soldiers. The more enterprising smokers amongst us are trying to persuade the non-smokers to use up their duty-free allowance of 200 Craven As in the red boxes with the black cat symbol.

Early one morning word gets round that we have

arrived. I jump out of my bunk and go on deck. We are in Southampton Water, which is gleaming faintly in the hazy, autumnal sunshine. Gradually, the coast becomes distinct. After the vast, monotonous, featureless and colourless expanses of the desert, there is this intense green, punctuated by a no less vivid red brick of rows of dolls' houses. There is also a profusion of brightly painted vehicles with large lettering on their sides: all so different from the endless columns of light-brown and green army trucks of Palestine.

Disembarkation is slow. We are at the end of the queue and, as friendly, but potentially troublesome aliens, we have to pass through screening by immigration officials. In the afternoon we board a well-upholstered toy-train, which steams through the lush meadows of Hampshire. London is a series of dark suburban stations, tunnels and glimpses of streets with red double-decker buses and trolley-buses. Out of London there are people bicycling on empty black tarmac roads which thread boldly through ripe wheat-fields spotted with red poppies. We pass slowly through a nondescript, sooty station, with a legendary name appearing enamelled white on a dark-blue background: CAMBRIDGE. But the colleges are nowhere to be seen.

It is late afternoon when we eventually stop at a tiny station in the middle of a forest. The pine trees reassure me that we are back in Europe at last. The presence of people selling the London-based *Polish Daily and Soldiers' Daily* indicates that Poland can't be too far away.

PART FOUR

England

(August 1947 – October 1952)

CHAPTER 14

England under the rain

At Brandon Station in Norfolk we climb into army trucks and start a long drive through dense but orderly woods with frequent 'Beware of Fire' notices along the roadside. We reach a clearing where there are far-flung rows of wooden huts. We have arrived at Bodney Airfield Camp. In the evening we queue for our first proper meal on British soil: a large tin of salmon for two, with no can opener in sight. We also get our first pay: half-a-crown to last us for ten days. We spend the increasingly chilly days playing poker, reading books, being drafted into jobs in the fields and railway sidings, and making blackberry wine, which ferments much too soon and explodes all over the ceiling. Poker is played in underground shelters, my job as junior is to sit above as look-out to warn of sergeant's approach. I collect sixpence for each game played.

Occasionally, we even have lessons, including some about the birds and the bees. Now and then chaps from the British Council arrive to explain the British way of life to us, as we gather in one of the huge hangars for assimilation lectures. One lecture is devoted to the

persistence and ubiquity of the horse as a source of
motive power on English roads. Throughout the camp
there are prominently displayed posters inviting us to
venture on a career in the coal n ines. I have two books
that I treasure: one is a gripping French novel (in Polish
translation) about the failed Polish uprising of 1863,
and the other is a beautiful illustrated edition of the
Economic History of England, by Charlotte Waters,
with engravings of the Spinning Jenny and satanic mills
and Gillray cartoons. I lose both to a bookish thief.

After some weeks father establishes contact with me.
He is now in a camp in Essex. Mother's transport has
ended up in Gloucestershire and my sister's in Surrey.
On 11 October 1947 father travels to Bodney Camp to
secure for me an honourable discharge from the Army
and takes me to Rivenhall, a big family camp near
Braintree, which we reach on a circuitous railway
journey via Norwich and Ipswich. In a dimly lit compartment, a woman offers me an orange, a luxury in
austerity Britain. She can't know that for the past five
years oranges have been part of my staple diet.

Months of boredom and discomfort follow at Rivenhall Camp. My parents and I are the proud occupants of
half a freezing Nissen hut, which we divide with
hanging blankets for privacy and ablutions in a zinc
tub. I go on excursions to Braintree by double-decker
bus to buy cans of paraffin for our stove. Through the
thin brick partition we can hear our semi-detached
neighbours and we get the full benefit from their radio
of a live commentary on the royal wedding of Elizabeth
and Philip. The other memorable social event is a visit
from one of my sister's many suitors, an excruciatingly
boring man who outstays his welcome and drives
mother to desperation.

Experiments with the zinc tub lead me to re-discover

Archimedes' Law. In order not to neglect my education completely, father asks a mathematics teacher in a nearby hut to instruct me in geometry and algebra, while another neighbour, a Jewish polymath, offers me volumes of his encyclopaedia to study. Professor Bębynek, the mathematician, is a brilliant teacher, lucid yet passionate. In contrast to ours, the interior of his hut is sparsely and neatly furnished and seems a reflection of his orderly mind. His trim wife sits quietly in the background.

Sadly, the mathematics tuition is soon ended. Father has found a way of escape from the camp. We collect our bundles and catch a train for Liverpool Street Station. A taxi takes us past the ruins surrounding St Paul's and across Waterloo Bridge made famous for me in a war-time film with a Polish theme. We then take another train into the heart of Royal Berkshire.

CHAPTER 15

Stateless persons in a stately home

We arrive in Bracknell on a frosty February evening and make our way into a nearby Victorian mansion. Morning light reveals the full splendour of Cooper's Hill. The three of us have taken possession of a spacious room with a huge Chippendale table and matching chairs, a large bay window overlooking a lawn, gravel paths and rose beds and, as far as the eye can see, a park full of trees and rhododendrons.

The estate is the property of a mysterious Pole who made his fortune smuggling gold in the Middle East using the facilities of the Polish Army. When British police invited him to help them with their enquiries, he deemed it prudent to depart for South America, leaving behind the sinister Mr Ropelewski as faithful administrator. Anxious to make the best use of the investment, he has packed every available space, including the servants' quarters and the gardener's house, with Polish refugees – on average two and half to a room. Next door we have Staś Kownacki, a young London University lecturer and his wife, who will eventually go to California; across the hall Zygmunt Górzewski, an army major, who before the war was an intelligence officer and adjutant to the President of the Republic, with his wife and daughter who will emigrate to Canada. Above us there is a bed-ridden old woman impatiently waiting for permission to join her son in the States (she is regarded with deep suspicion by the other residents on account of her contacts with diplomats from People's Poland); an elderly couple in a room above us; another younger couple with a son – the parents look grim and eventually commit suicide; a family with three little children on the way to Brazil; Major Kopel, victim of Soviet labour camps, who keeps fighting the Polish 1939 campaign, with wife and two teenage children; Mr Geissler, a dashing young bachelor and secretive poet fated to die young of cancer; Jan Rostworowski, a poetry-writing count, owner of a mobile delicatessen store, with two babes and a bumptious wife who tries to bully me into kissing her hand and addressing her as 'Countess'; soon he will dazzle the Polish London establishment with yards of effortlessly composed rubbish (many years later he will improve somewhat, maybe as a result of my savage criticisms); Mr and Mrs Wanke, a middle-aged couple who cultivate the extensive kitchen garden: he is President of the Polish Farmers' Union, while she paints, is full of cultural zeal and, noticing my incipient interest in art, sends me off to the National Gallery in London with instructions to look at a handful of named pictures by Mantegna, Botticelli, El Greco, Velázquez, Poussin, Titian, Rembrandt, Constable, Turner and Cézanne, and ignore everything else. This is certainly an improvement on school art lessons, during which we spend hours imitating a garrulous ancient interminably patching up his painting of a rhododendron bush. My passion for the visual arts is established. In an unguarded moment I tell Mrs Wanke that I have started writing poetry. She insists on seeing these first efforts but I am diffident and stubborn enough to resist. She also tries to bully my sister into preferring Bach to pop songs, but is equally unsuccessful.

Zosia is now only a visitor at Cooper's Hill: she is studying medicine at the Royal College of Surgeons in Dublin. Father had employed all his boundless energies into finding her a university place in England, but all the institutions are crowded with demobbed soldiers and the idea of offering a place to a woman who wants to be a surgeon doesn't seem all that attractive to admissions tutors. He fails to place me in any of the equally overcrowded Catholic public schools and I am enrolled at the local school just across the road, with a strong Church of England bias under its soon-to-be-ordained-in-late-middle-age headmaster. Ranelagh School turns out to be one of those then rare and delectable establishments, a co-educational grammar school, where the girls offer us boys models of diligence and good behaviour, and chances to examine the stronger sex at close range.

[My sister has preserved the letters I wrote to her from Bracknell while she was studying in Dublin. They are a mixture of somewhat strained schoolboy humour, quotations and passages in Latin and English, and various mystifications; more seriously, they record my growing absorption in literature (English and Polish, particularly in Shakespeare, Byron, Słowacki and Norwid), my love of the Classics, my hero worship of Julius Caesar; musical discoveries, particularly of Chopin's music which is given a new impetus during the 1949 centenary celebrated in great style by the

BBC; advice on which radio programmes she should listen to.

I report my admiration for the film *Forever Amber* and inform her that we as a class had condemned Jane Austen's *Pride and Prejudice* as 'dull and daft'. I ask her to bring me a skull and I offer her my body for dissection for £20 if she is short of cash. I quote corny one-liners like 'I bought a new boomerang but I have some difficulty in throwing the old one away', probably culled from *Everybody's Weekly* and *The Reader's Digest*. What she really thought of all this I now have no idea as I have not preserved her letters to me.

Extracts from these letters are quoted in this and the two final chapters.]

Despite my initial reaction ('I've now been going to school for two days, but it's difficult because we have French and Latin, and in addition English is difficult. Anyway, to hell with all learning!'), it is a great relief to be involved in the English educational system again, though, as I discover, at Ranelagh the system is suffering from a post-war debility. Moreover, the results of my sporadic and chaotic schooling so far are difficult to integrate with the standard curriculum, and the need to catch up on my Latin sends me on weekly trips all the way to Streatham for lessons from the former head-mistress of my Polish school in Tel Aviv. She is a remarkable teacher, but her husband, a distinguished pre-war banker, turns out to be surprisingly incompetent at personal money management and succumbs to the wiles of a conman. Relieved of all their savings, they hang themselves in their living room.

In those days Bracknell was still a quiet little Victorian red-brick town on the edge of fashionable Ascot where I catch a glimpse of waxen-faced George VI being driven past a cheering crowd in a landau. Not yet designated a new town, it has no national weather centre and no jazz festival, it hasn't even a public library, and the formidable Racal Engineering has only just been established.

The meagre school library, whose nucleus consists of dilapidated nineteenth-century tomes of church history, fascinating Germanic investigations into the *Urquelle*, the source of St Mark's Gospel, and Gilbert Murray's flabby fin-de-siècle translations of Greek plays, is now slowly being supplemented with exciting volumes of poetry by Eliot, Yeats and Wilfred Owen, as well as a new life of naughty Algernon Swinburne. There is Lytton Strachey's dazzling introduction to French literature and a history of the subject by an American academic who dismisses Proust as an aberration on account of his unmanageable sentences and clumsy punctuation.

Mr Smith, my English master, has a great passion for poetry; his nickname is 'Basher', but although he can be quite violent with the unruly mobsters, he is tolerant and understanding with pupils who are willing to learn. He is happy to be persuaded by me that we should study Browning rather than Tennyson. One of the books we read in class is T. E. Lawrence's *Seven Pillars of Wisdom*. Here I come into my own as resident Arabist, basking in glory as Mr Smith's consultant. He is also relentless in his championship of correct English usage and engages in endless skirmishes with our misrelated participles and misplaced 'onlys'.

Mr Longfield-Jones, the other English master, is even more fastidious in his zeal for syntactical purity. He also takes us for Religious Knowledge. He is wiry and mercurial, with ginger hair, heavy horn-rimmed spectacles, he carries a bamboo cane which he smacks against his gown; he has a squeaky voice which turns into a leery smile when he happens upon a passage of Kings or Chronicles redolent of lechery or excessive violence. His eyebrows twitch in imitation of Groucho Marx. He is the cause of my enduring loathing for the Old Testament. He is popular with some of the naughtier girls, who giggle at his frequent and irrational references to James Mason. I catch a glimpse of him some twenty years later, when we both file out of a British Academy lecture in London. His red hair is now silvery at the edges.

Mr Berry, the headmaster, is ineffective and wimpish; his reputation is not enhanced by his wife who on her rare, accidental appearances looks wild and scatty and calls him 'Bim'. But he is a wonderful teacher of Latin. Many happy hours are spent on Julius Caesar's gripping account of his campaigns in Britain, on the elegance of Horace's *Odes* and Virgil's sombre epic. His approach to religious studies is markedly different from that practised by Mr Longfield-Jones: it is a serious discussion of Patristic thought. In a moment of weakness I confess to him that I would like to become a cleric, albeit a Catholic one. I have my eye on the Papacy, though more in the spirit of Nietzschean Will to Power than of Christian humility and service.

Miss Gertrude Hanna is Mr Berry's Deputy. She has been teaching science at the school since the First World War but gives the impression that she specialises in alchemy and pre-Newtonian physics, gives that impression, that is, when she is allowed to be heard by the mob. No wonder the class is eventually united in the experience of total failure in O-level science. When the school is taken to the local cinema to see Olivier's *Hamlet* and hears the King's agonised 'Oh Gertrude! Gertrude!', it greets his pain with a roar of laughter to the great bewilderment and annoyance of the rest of the audience. ('*Hamlet*, which I have read only twice, I remembered so well that I knew what would happen next and even what would be said by whom. I was only curious to see how the scenes would be presented. That ghost was so abominably staged that even I wasn't frightened, but otherwise the film was quite passable. Unfortunately the only drawback was hunger which increased steadily since my "modest" breakfast and became impossibly irritating at 5.00 by the time Hamlet was being carried away on that stretcher.')

Mr Strawson's lessons in geometry and algebra are impeccable, as are the figures he draws on the blackboard, helping himself with the edge of his gown to compose perfect circles. His colleague, on the other hand, a small excitable man, whose name I forget, has a very tough time with his boring accountant's arithmetic.

The ancient Mr Beare teaches singing and also gives me private piano lessons. He is the classic sadist who hurts me deeply both when he ridicules my piano playing and when he singles me out in front of the whole class as the disadvantaged bloody foreigner who by his diligence and application has surpassed the rest of them.

Being an English school, it is of course sports and games mad. Many hours are wasted in diving into icy pools, chasing variously sized balls in muddy fields and running cross-country on foggy autumnal afternoons. Nevertheless, I manage to gain a certain reputation in this domain. As a Suez Canal veteran I perform well in swimming; at other times luck and cunning help. In the mile run I am proclaimed victor: I have fallen so far behind that the referee doesn't spot that I am ahead of the pack only because I have run one lap fewer than everybody else. On a cross-country run on a murky afternoon I lead a few friends through a hole in the fence of the Cooper's Hill estate, gaining a good half mile's advantage. As we sit panting in the changing room, Mr Ware admires my performance and tells me that apparently a group of boys had taken a short cut through the grounds of my home. My face registers disbelief and outrage at this unsporting behaviour.

Mr Ware is the history master. He drives a dark-green MG and has a fondness for disciplinarian gym. He is nevertheless an old-fashioned liberal, who teaches us about the benign effects on the world of British imperial rule, and about the great statesmanship of Lloyd George, who wisely opposed the shabby treatment of Germany under the Versailles Treaty. This is too much for a patriotic Pole like me, who knows that the devious Welshman had favoured the Germans at the expense of the newly formed Polish state, whose geographical location he only dimly understood. Regular classroom battles ensue, as I am also startled to see Napoleon, the great champion of liberty, turned into an evil adventurer. I think back to those noble pictures of the Napoleonic campaigns in our Warsaw flat, of Polish Napoleonic regiments fighting gallantly for universal freedom in Italy, Spain, Russia and the West Indies. I recall Victor Hugo's epic description of the great disaster at Waterloo in *Les Misérables*. I am equally distressed that the legendary Polish heroes, Kościuszko and Pułaski, who so significantly contributed to the success of the American War of Independence, are not even mentioned in my textbook, and that the brave Americans, led by George Washington, are depicted as a band of obdurate colonials mishandled by Lord North and George III. Having also read in a Polish translation that exciting adventure story of the plucky Boer farmers resisting British military might, I come painfully to realise that the past is much more difficult to know than the future.

I am no less dismayed to learn that no one has heard about the great Polish poet Adam Mickiewicz, who, I know, is as good as Shakespeare, whom I have just been discovering from little sixpenny editions of *Julius Caesar* and *Macbeth*, and from my first experiences of professional theatre: *The Merchant of Venice* in Reading, followed by visits to the Old Vic to see Olivier, Dorothy Tutin and Paul Rogers in other Shakespeare plays. This cultural parochialism of the British stimulates me to start translating Polish literature, and my first clumsy rendering of a poem by Cyprian Norwid appears in the school magazine. My rapturous account of a production of a Polish play by émigrés in London earns a special commendation from Mr Smith.

('The advantage I derived from seeing Słowacki's plays on stage did not end with a satiation of the moral need of my sensitive mind etc., etc., I also had a great material advantage. A week *post factum opportunissimus* we had a subject set for an essay: "Write a letter to your aunt describing your last visit to the theatre." At once I saw the propaganda *possibilitas* and informed my "aunt" from A to Z. For this I got 17/20 (the first time ever!) with the comment "An excellent piece of work – see Mr Bury [the headmaster]." Added was a pencil comment "Can't you Poles all be called Smith?". Słowacki, Nowakowski etc., that was too much for him. But do not think, oh mortal creature, that I intend to boast (nobody knows this apart from you). May Zeus's thunder burn me, may Caesar stop regarding me as one who dares pay homage to him if I lie. I am convinced it is one of the Muses, the admirers of the handsome Juliusz (not Caesar [but Słowacki]), had forgotten to chase him to Elysium, so she stayed to uphold his fame, to praise his greatness through my lips. If you've understood what this last sentence is all about, let me know.')

[I proceed to tell Zosia that a new Słowacki has appeared in our midst – I too am writing a tragedy, though I discover that I have nothing much to say after the first few sentences and therefore think I now understand why so many Romantic tragedies were left unfinished.]

CHAPTER 16

Enlightenment in the air

The major source of my enlightenment proves to be the BBC Third Programme and the Home Service. However, as we live in one room, listening is not easy. ('I did listen to *Lear* for a while but my nerves were giving up so I switched over to *Take It From Here*.') Time has to be allowed for mother's piano playing, for father's singing and writing and, when she is home on vacation, for my sister's tuning in to Radio Warsaw. Moreover, father is apprehensive about the frequent radio adaptations of Strindberg and Ibsen – whom he remembers as causing scandal at the turn of the century in Kraków, which was both the bastion of respectability and the hotbed of modernism in literature and art – but his grasp of English is mercifully not good enough to control my listening. There is an epic production of *Peer Gynt* with Grieg's music, of *Ghosts, Hedda Gabler, An Enemy of the People, Rosmersholm, The Father* and *Creditors*. There are also strange and wonderful radio plays like *Childe Roland to the Dark Tower Came* by Louis MacNeice and an adaptation of a vigorous Strindberg fairy tale.

However, father feels on firmer ground when he bans Bartók's 'cacophonic' *Music for Strings, Percussion and Celesta* and Handel's operas, which he is convinced damage the human voice, an organ whose natural purpose is to articulate the melodies of Fauré, Tosti, Karłowicz and Leoncavallo. But the Chopin centenary in 1949, lavishly commemorated by the *Radio Times* and the Third Programme, unites the family briefly. The *Radio Times* publishes my letter of thanks for this Polish celebration and father is indignant that he has to learn about this momentous event from our letter-page reading butcher rather than from me. This is also the occasion for our first visit to the plush warm intimacies of the Wigmore Hall in London to hear Józef Turczyński, mother's pre-war teacher and co-editor with Paderewski of Chopin's works, give a couple of recitals. Turczyński, who lives quietly in Switzerland, is not an international celebrity, so the first recital is not well attended. But his mastery is soon recognised and people struggle to get tickets for his second appearance. His self-effacement was such that even the *Grove Dictionary of Music* fails to record his name.

('Dearest Zosia!

' "Creeping unwillingly like a snail to school" – Shakespeare!).

'Yesterday I got bored and depressed so I went to Reading – with £1 in my pocket! – and visited a bookshop where I found a nice book about Chopin in the Master Musicians series – almost new with Delacroix's portrait for 3/6, that is 4/- cheaper than in a shop. I also went to see *Hold That Baby* with the Bowery Boys – If you don't know it, I advise you to go for a good laugh.')

With its theatres, concert halls and galleries London is my promised land, but in the country I have to rely on the radio, books bought by post, Polish classics sent by the Polish Library in London and correspondence course scripts sent to me by a sympathetic tutor in Glasgow who treats with equanimity my hostile revaluations of the giants of Polish literature. Amongst Zosia's medical texts I find Freud on dreams and the Oedipus complex, and these discoveries make a profound impression. The surrounding countryside I discover pedalling on an ancient recalcitrant bicycle.

Our Berkshire retreat is disturbed when Ernest Bevin, His Majesty's Principal Secretary for Foreign Affairs, invites us all to go home, now that Stalin has re-established independent Poland. Bevin already has a secure place in Polish demonology as the trade unionist who had led British dockers in denying vital supplies to Poland during its struggle with the Red Army in 1920. So when he sends out officials to put pressure on every single Pole in the country to return to Poland, his initiative is contemptuously dismissed as another example of the chronic British inability to understand the Soviet menace. Fresh anxieties about our future are raised in the face of this latest example of British perfidy in dealing with Poles.

The Cold War is now freezing everything in sight. As I report in a letter written to Zosia at about this time, I heard or read an announcement from Prague by M. Kursal, Chairman of the Czechoslovak School Textbook Committee, to the effect that 'The princes of the fairy tales will no longer be examples for our children. Instead, the characters will be modelled on our great President Klement Gottwald and on our shock and brigade workers.' That inspired my own impromptu contribution in English which I included in my letter:

'Hullo children ! Once upon a time there lived a girl whose name was Little Red (not to be confused, of course, with the Miss Riding Hood led astray by the Capitalist wolf in the Western plutocracies). Now, one day, Little Red was sitting alone in her cell, because her two Ugly Sisters, Titonia and Trotsky True, had gone to the Stakhanovite ball. Then in came Fairy Godfather Joseph, and when she produced her Party card he whisked her away to that hall in an armoured car he produced with a wave of his wand from a collective farm pumpkin.

'As the clock struck twelve Little Red had to rush back home and she left her glass slipper behind because some Fascist beast tripped her on the stairs. She was also very late because that reactionary Herbert Morrison had turned the clock to Double Summer Time.

'Next day the handsome Prince Klement went all over the land seeking the wearer of the slipper. Titonia and Trotsky True dared not show their ugly feet behind the Iron Curtain, but only Little Red's foot was the right size. "Comrade!" said the Prince, and they lived happily for five years according to Plan.'

[The letter continues in Polish]

'I had a happy day today because I went to Reading and saw *Hamlet* and took the opportunity to go to that same bookshop where I found the biography of Caesar as well as all Byron's works in one volume for a mere 2/6 !!!!

'I did listen to Chopin but not right to the end because Father wanted to sleep.'

Meanwhile father, sitting in his Chippendale chair facing the bay window and the park beyond, dreams of making a fortune, or at least a little extra money. He composes crossword puzzles and pompous leaders for the *Polish Daily* in London (which are duly rejected), he fills in football coupons and, reviving his pre-war schemes, dreams up inventions intended to make the work in the home and the office more agreeable and more efficient. He enlists me as his translator. It is an excruciating job. His documentation has to be turned into English legal jargon and his correspondence, couched in effusive, circumlocutory Polish, has to be rendered into meaningful, sober, yet courteous English. But father is a firm believer in absolute precision and it is only with the greatest reluctance, and following acrimonious arguments, that he allows me to translate phrases like 'And I remain for ever in your debt and sign myself with due respect and gratitude' as, 'Yours faithfully. . .'

These ventures lose father a lot of money he doesn't have. Mother is growing increasingly nervous and apprehensive; she keeps reminding him of his reckless-ness with money in Warsaw and his readiness to part with it either to pursue a quixotic scheme or to support a devious friend. There is mysterious talk of a lender in London who is becoming impatient. A bright idea occurs to me. I slip out of the house to a nearby telephone booth and call Cooper's Hill. Mother answers the phone and I tell her in a menacing impatient voice that I want to speak to her husband about that outstanding debt. She rushes off in panic and I in panic ring off. I slip back into the family room to find my parents and Zosia in a conclave of bitter recrimination. I am unable to maintain my composure and my shrewd sister soon tumbles on to the truth. I might have been in deep trouble, but there is so much relief and amusement that I am allowed to get away with it.

Mr Ropelewski now persuades father to invest more money he doesn't have in a brood of newly-hatched ducklings. Father, the epitome of a city man, can now be seen in his three-piece suit chasing after the ducklings all over the park. The birds flourish, grow rapidly and then rapidly and inexplicably die off, hundreds of them. But father's trust in the administrator remains undiminished, for Mr Ropelewski is a Marshal Piłsudski loyal veteran, and such people are above suspicion. Mother, however, is now equally confirmed in her view that a man who could send back to communist hell his gentle, aristocratic but dotty wife is a scoundrel.

So perhaps it's not surprising that one of my letters to Zosia contains the following, mischievous portrait of father, composed in English.

> Dear Madam,
>   We are looking for a man who has the following (though how rare!) features: he must have inventive talents notably in the field of broom manufacture and 'go slow' office furniture (for go slow strikes) and a commanding personality. If moreover the aforesaid character had a baritone voice, was an admirer of the great Lithuanian King George Pilsuzzchy, disliked the music of Sibelius, positively believed that war with Russia was inevitable and had no command of spoken English, we are prepared to offer him the directorship of our Firm at a salary of £3,000 p.a. (Income Tax £4,000). Awaiting your reply is your grateful and humble servant. . .

But Mr Ropelewski hasn't got much life left in him, and neither has Cooper's Hill. The mansion slowly empties as more and more people move out and seek their fortunes overseas or hang themselves in despair. The County Council takes possession of the property and sends gratuitously threatening eviction notices to those few, like us, still remaining. The solicitor's letter, as I am to learn from years of experience, typifies the legal mind's view of justice: that a person is presumed guilty until proved insane. As the family's principal secretary and translator responsible for drafting a reply, I feel deeply humiliated.

CHAPTER 17

Two moves add up to one fire

Father takes the view that while I am still at school, we should stay in the locality before trying our luck in London. So we examine details of properties available for rent in Royal Berkshire. They all turn out to be sumptuous residences with mahogany sideboards stuffed with family silver, whose owners are temporarily out of the country holidaying in the south of France or governing Hong Kong. So we take up the Council's offer of a hut in a camp in a wood on the edge of a pig farm where people who were evacuated from London during the blitz and have not found the energy to move out, still live. Father takes a night-shift job at the Huntley & Palmers biscuit factory in Reading and mother one on the day-shift. They pass each other morning and evening as they walk some five miles to and from Bracknell railway station next to Cooper's Hill now needlessly vacant. I report to Zosia:

13 Warfield Camp, 15 April 1951

Dear Sister,
The black clouds have thundered by, the

cataclysms have ceased and we have landed in
the peace and quiet of a God-forsaken dump
next to which Bracknell seems like a real town.
Namely on Tuesday we have landed in Arcady
where, though the country is pastoral, instead of
shepherds blowing their pipes, there is a crowd of
screaming kids, barking dogs and mooing cows
which for no apparent reason moo only at night.
As you must be guessing by now we are living in
a three-room stone barrack which on account of
the temperature it registers in the morning could
easily be called a fridge. Through the small
prison windows we perceive the colourful and
familiar view of Nissen huts in late-Gothic style.

An hour before leaving [Cooper's Hill] I went to
the park for silent contemplation in this garden,
the last neglected and deserted seat of
degenerated gentry. The sun appeared for a
moment and a Romantic atmosphere entered
this springtime park. A pity I had to leave it so
young.

But mother is delighted that the rent is only 7/6d a
week and she can play the piano without disturbing
anyone. I have a room to myself. A little cuddly black
cat strays, joins the household and keeps me warm at
night. I am now studying hard beneath a roaring gas
light. Badly advised at school about university entrance,
I have to prepare for an additional A-level in Latin,
which means working my way through Livy's elliptically
composed history all on my own in half the normal
time, and I also have to keep up some six O-level
courses postponed by a year on account of my youth.
Were it not for the ubiquitous mud, the desolate
appearance of the huts, and the pig stench carried on

the prevailing wind, our conditions would seem as good as those at Cooper's Hill, and we even have a kitchen to ourselves, with a gas cooker that nearly kills me the night I have to sleep there when my brother-in-law comes on a visit and mother doesn't quite turn the stove off.

Our faithful bakelite Pye radio had given up the ghost at Cooper's Hill and would in any event have been useless at Warfield Camp. Somehow I have acquired a radio the size of a bedside cupboard powered by two huge liquid batteries that have to be taken once a week (hanging precariously from my bicycle's handlebars) to a shop in Bracknell for a 24-hour recharging. This is the time when I am discovering Mozart operas, which are being relayed from the Salzburg Festival, and I dread the possibility of the batteries giving up in the middle of a performance. Could I even have dreamt that within months of taking up my first job (in Munich) I would be travelling to Salzburg to hear *Don Giovanni*?

Although mother continues to see me as the obvious successor to Paderewski and Rubinstein, I know my limitations and in any event my ambition is to read English at Oxford, so that I can become the *Observer* drama critic in succession to Ivor Brown and go to all those wonderful London theatres every night of the week. My passion for Oxford was born early but I don't know how or why. Probably father, a great believer in the glories of academic excellence, provided the inspiration. But Ranelagh, with no experience of sending candidates to the ancient universities, and not much experience of sending them to any other centres of learning either, confines its guidance to instructions about how to reach The High from Oxford Railway Station. So I seek out the overwhelmingly uninformative Oxford Calendar and naturally opt for the three oldest Colleges: University, Balliol and Merton. Merton invites me to sit the entrance exam. At the Lodge I ask to see the Warden. I reach his study on the first floor: the door is wide open and the large windows of the opulent room display a vista of Christ Church Meadows. Luckily, Geoffrey Mure, the resident Hegelian, is not around and I have time to reflect that it would be better for me not to seek an interview with him just yet. Back at the Lodge I am allotted a suite of rooms overlooking the cobbled Merton Street on the one side and the Front Quad on the other. The study is lined with fearsomely learned books, mostly annotated texts of Greek classics, and my regret at not being allowed to take Greek at school is reinforced. This enchanted residence, now briefly vacated over Easter for my benefit, belongs to a Mr John Adlard. The name of this legendary being stays in my mind. When over thirty years later I take up residence as a writing Fellow at Hawthornden Castle I see his name again on a door next to mine, registering his Fellowship during a previous session there.

Oxford is everything I hoped for and imagined, even though at breakfast I am nauseated by porridge and kippers and stunned by the proliferating silver cutlery, some of it shaped into forms I have never seen before. When chatting to the boys in competition with me I notice that they are well above the Ranelagh average but I display enough self-confidence to persuade them that my Polish way of pronouncing 'John Donne', a name I hadn't previously come across, is the correct one. After the two-day exam I wait in an ante-chamber to the interview room, whose walls are covered with Max Beerbohm's cartoons, which I recognise from my readings of illustrated articles in *Everybody's Weekly*, a magazine sadly long since defunct, which was always packed with fascinating contributions on ancient history, religion and the arts, always ready for any excuse to celebrate Sir Max's work and sometimes ready to publish my letters in defence of the Polish case in the arts or history.

The interview board of some twelve Fellows, headed by the Warden and J. R. R. Tolkien, bearing down from behind an interminably long green-baize covered table, offers me no chance to display my familiarity with Sir Max or any other aspect of cultural history. I am advised to spend another year at school before trying again but I know that another year there would be unendurable. I have exhausted its academic and intellectual potential; the girl I wanted to take to the theatre in London had reversed her acceptance of my invitation on her mother's advice, so all the girls at school have suddenly lost their charm; two of my close friends, Scott, a lover of music and poetry, left after O-levels, as did Foster, my great rival in solving quadratic equations and obviously a very talented mathematician, who is not allowed to stay on by his unenterprising parents. Their faces and voices are still with me, but their Christian names are lost. Robert Stubbs had moved on to further study in London. He will remain my only link with the school until his premature and lonely death from heart attack on a deserted beach in Kenya in 1973.

My consolation prize is the County Scholarship and offer of a place at Reading University following a competitive exam there. I see the prospect of a glittering career in the metropolis receding, when I am summoned for a late interview at King's College London. As I walk along the Embankment I notice a tram crowded with people waving banners and balloons. It's on its last voyage before giving way to the bus. The admissions tutor, the mountainous, sybaritic D. M. Low, editor of

Gibbon's *Decline and Fall* and friend of Norman
Douglas who wrote *Siren Land* and *South Wind*, is
impressed with my knowledge of Byron's *Don Juan*,
which, he tells me, no English schoolboy reads. That
proves enough for him to offer me a place. These
schoolboys don't know what they are missing.

Our riches-to-rags-to-elegance-to-rags story takes
another turn as we now move out of the boggy pig-
infested Berkshire camp into a hotel off Kensington
High Street, via a short sojourn in a bedsit in Putney.
Mother reiterates the proverb 'Two moves add up to
one fire': in this fire I lose my dilapidated but wonderfully comprehensive bound edition of Gustav Doré's
engravings. Father has been appointed hotel manager
by the Polish Ex-Combatants' Association. A sociable
organisation-man he has at last found an ideal employment. He begins his purposeful task of reviving this
ailing investment by chasing out the prostitutes and the
doddery resident drunks and redecorating its thirty
rooms. Soon, business is booming. That will prove too
much for the Association which will decide it is prudent
to sell a prospering investment and send father into
retirement into dismal Shepherd's Bush, where a
devious house agent had persuaded him to buy an
uneconomic bedsit property.

Meanwhile, my boundless pride and excitement at
becoming a university student, confirmed by the
purchase of the College scarf, generously financed by
mother, are not dampened by the young tutor Miss
Emmy Taylor, fresh from Dr Leavis's Cambridge, who
demonstrates to me in the first week of term that the
London University English syllabus I am so eager to
study, has been devised by disgraceful academic
frauds, who have no faith in their own discipline,
perceiving it as a second-rate substitute for studying

the Classics. Undeterred, I stay the course, but the lesson sinks in.

As past Head Boy and winner of the County Scholarship, I return to Ranelagh on Speech Day to collect my Sixth Form Arts Prize from Sir John Wolfenden, then Vice-Chancellor of Reading University. In his report the headmaster boasts that a boy had achieved the unbelievable *97 per cent* in an O-level arts subject exam. The sly old devil doesn't let on it was me getting it for a paper in Polish Language and Literature. On my final school report he had written: 'He has had an excellent school career. I wish him well in the future.'

Meanwhile, my ambition to study at Oxford smoulders on and will eventually be satisfied some years later when I go up to Trinity College to do postgraduate work in Philosophy. When, shortly before his death, Geoffrey Mure reads a paper at the Royal Institute of Philosophy in London, I find it difficult to concentrate on the argument as I stare at his bald head, listen to the beguiling music of his mandarin voice and am both haunted by ancient memories and marvel at the tenacious survival of this successor to F. H. Bradley, an object of scorn in post-idealist Oxford.

CONCLUSION

Houses and homes

A consequence of surviving to middle age is that one can look back on the past from a new, at times a very poignant perspective. There is the, as it were, mental and spiritual perspective which issues in autobiographical exercises like the present one. There is also simply and straightforwardly a physical perspective. One may, that is, just be fortunate or unfortunate enough to be faced with an opportunity to revisit the places one has known as a child. Such opportunities appear the more dramatic, the more remote and inaccessible those places are.

In recent years I have been in such a position.

I have been revisiting Warsaw often since 1963. I always make a point of walking down Nowogrodzka Street past the modernist Post Office, ending up in the rebuilt Baroque St Barbara's church. On the way I pass a side street linking Nowogrodzka Street with Aleje Jerozolimskie at a point leading almost directly to the Central Station at the far side of the Aleje. The houses in this side street are dark, grim and pockmarked with bullets and shrapnel. They are among the few that survived the 1939 air raids and the 1944 Uprising. But the adjoining part of Nowogrodzka has not survived: our house is gone. Gone too are the rails which brought the suburban railway almost to our door. Somehow, I never summoned enough energy to seek out aunt Janka's villa in the suburbs. Perhaps this is because my time is always better spent in her company in her tiny flat a few minutes' walk from Nowogrodzka Street.

But of my recent return journeys the one to the Holy Land was the one most laden with significance. The place was not only remote in time, it was also remote in space and I did not forsee a chance to travel there: the opportunity came unexpectedly in 1987.

There was no point in searching the deserts for signs of our camp. I had no idea where to look for the building which had housed St George's in Jaffa – assuming it had not disappeared in the cordon sanitaire the Israelis have created along the borderline between Tel Aviv and Jaffa. But Collège St Joseph was known to my Tel Aviv taxi driver who also remembered the Polish war-time presence. We stopped outside a small well-proportioned building in the French colonial style, protected by railings. It was July, so the school was shut and empty and quiet, but I could just peer into the central corridor with a glimpse of the playground beyond. How diminutive my childhood Escorial had become! The clutter of buildings next door no longer advertised itself as a girls' school.

The monastic St Peter's Church on the promontory overlooking Jaffa port and visible across the bay from Tel Aviv now stood amid tourist shops, boutiques, restaurants and high-quality housing built in a traditional local style. Preparations for a rock concert were loudly in progress in public gardens nearby. This was no longer the smelly, overcrowded ruinous Jaffa I have known – this was a chic 'old' Tel Aviv constructed as a foil to the anonymous modern city. This church where father sang now stood barred against me: I was wearing shorts. I watched with frustration as the tourist in front of me went back to put on a pair of trousers he had ready in the boot of his car. Arabs still dominated the streets away from the promontory, so the old atmosphere was briefly recaptured as I made my way back to Tel Aviv on foot.

Naturally what I most wanted to see was the spot in Hajarkon where our little house had stood. I walked up Ben-Yehuda now looking much narrower and less grand, and turned into Frishman. The big trees which provided so much desirable shade were gone. But at the crossroads with Hajarkon there on the right-hand corner stood – I realised after a moment with amazement and delight – the old house! Not instantly recognisable because of its disguise: the exuberance of the façade had been severely toned down and decorators were actually in the process of repainting it gleaming white with a light blue central riband: like an approximation of the Israeli flag. In case I might have had any doubts that this was the same building, I was able to reassure myself when I peered into its familiar L-shaped courtyard: it still had the original paint and general appearance but was in a state of severe dilapidation. The mysterious twin villa across the road was also there but boarded up, its formal garden now neglected. All those neighbouring villas and apartment blocks which looked so superior in the forties, were now suffering from a leprous decay.

The encounters in Jerusalem were less dramatic. As expected, the Old City still stands as it did then, and so does St George's and its tuck shop tucked into the school's perimeter wall, and so does its neo-gothic chapel-cathedral. I stood for a while in the junior playground: the street behind me, the colonnaded walkway in front, the dormitories, somewhat shrunk, to the right, the classrooms to the left. Again my piano teacher playing Chopin came to haunt me. It was time to move on.

I had spent the first important childhood years in Palestine and I went back there in search of a house which, in the unlikely event that it was still standing, would have the distinction of being my earliest identifiable home. It is probably because my Warsaw home was destroyed that my identification with the Polish capital is somehow less emotional, more symbolic. Overall, Palestine and Lebanon are the memorable lands of my childhood. Life in Poland, partly because it covered my very early years, partly because it was in its closing phase so violent and disrupted, belongs to my pre-history. So in an important sense Palestine and Lebanon are my native lands, now in memory purged of the fears and anxieties that I had to endure at the time. But Palestine too was a violent land, increasingly so towards the end of my stay, the seeds of the great conflicts to come were being sown. The destruction of Lebanon came later and I watched from a distance the agony of this idyllic sanctuary with growing horror and sadness.

So in August 1947 England, quiet, orderly, somewhat old-fashioned and somnolent, immediately appealed to me as the haven of stability and normality which had been eluding me since September 1939.

Yet, ironically, it was Bracknell, my English 'home town', which had undergone the most radical change. It was to be expected that the extensive grounds of Cooper's Hill would be converted into a residential estate of modern brick boxes, so it was a pleasant surprise to see that the mansion itself was not bulldozed. But it was the wholesale conversion of this Victorian township into a grid of tatty skyscrapers resembling a small American city, surrounded by a busy ring road, which was sufficient to bring on me a severe attack of alienation when in 1987 I revisited my old school on Founder's Day. I went too late: of the two teachers I most wanted to see, Mr Smith, the English master, had just died, while Mr Ware the historian was too ill to attend.

The most elusive and tantalising of all these is mother's home in the Ukraine, which I had never seen and which she will never see again, but which she kept recreating for herself and for us in words. One of my earliest poems, called 'Home' and dedicated to her, attempts a celebration of that mythical dwelling and its ambience.

Having tried to make so many places feel like home, it was not surprising that when, after a poetry reading in a school near Warsaw, a pupil asked, 'Don't you feel nostalgic for the old country?' I had to reply, 'As I have recently moved from Gloucestershire in the west of England to Kent in the east, I currently feel nostalgic for the Gloucestershire countryside.'

Founded in 1986, Serpent's Tail publishes the innovative and the challenging.

If you would like to receive a catalogue of our current publications please write to:

FREEPOST
Serpent's Tail
4 Blackstock Mews
LONDON N4 2BR

(No stamp necessary if your letter is posted in the United Kingdom.)